# MUNCIE
## MURDER & MAYHEM

DOUGLAS WALKER & KEITH ROYSDON

THE
History
PRESS

Published by The History Press
Charleston, SC
www.historypress.com

*Front cover, top*: Muncie Newspapers; *bottom*: Ball State University Digital Archives.
*Back cover (badge)*: Ball State University Digital Archives; *bottom*: photo by Keith Roysdon.

First published 2018

Manufactured in the United States

ISBN 9781467138901

Library of Congress Control Number: 2017963916

# CONTENTS

Introduction                                          5

1. The City Everyone Shunned                          7
2. Jules LaDuron's Early Years                        15
3. Waiting for Harry Bateman                          22
4. Mountain Justice                                   26
5. George Dale vs. the KKK                            32
6. "The Luckiest Guy in the World"                    40
7. The Disappearance of Freda LaDuron                 49
8. The Meat Market Murder                             56
9. Jules LaDuron and the Carter Brothers              63
10. Enter at Your Own Risk                            72
11. The Cops Who Wouldn't Stop                        79
12. The Death of Innocents                            83
13. A Mother's Love                                   88
14. Murder in the Classroom                           97
15. Life Is Cheap                                     105
16. To Protect…and to Steal                           110
17. Jules LaDuron, His Final Years                    115

Bibliography                                          119
Index                                                 125
About the Authors                                     127

# INTRODUCTION

Like many cities, Muncie, Indiana, has its light side and its dark side. The dark side is a place where murder is committed, where heinous acts are carried out against the defenseless and innocent. It is where hate dwells.

The light side is where good men and women work hard and play hard but sometimes fall victim to the darkest urges of those around them. When that happens, police and prosecutors move to see justice done.

Sometimes, that split between light and dark, good and evil, hero and villain, is a matter of perspective. Depending on where you stand, as well as your understanding of a person and their history, they can seem to be dastardly or heroic.

There is no better example in Muncie's history than Jules LaDuron, a figure of legend in the city. LaDuron's life spanned much of the twentieth century and some of its most notorious events, including the still-unsolved disappearance of his wife and the night two men came to his medical office with menace in mind.

While LaDuron's life can be reduced to a few milestones of violence and death, he was much more: a physician, a sportsman, a loving grandfather, a member of Muncie's pioneering NFL team and a man remembered by neighbors for his kindness and caring for others.

Another Muncie figure of legend is one of LaDuron's contemporaries, George Dale, a newspaper publisher and one-time mayor. Dale was known for the political battles he waged through his newspaper, but his legend lives on for his fight against the Ku Klux Klan, a fight waged at risk to his own life.

This book tells true stories of legends like LaDuron and Dale, but also people whose only fame came when their names were splashed across newspaper pages in lurid headlines, when photos showed—in black and white—the pools of blood where their bodies lay.

These were people made victims in Muncie's smallpox epidemic; those cut down in the city's dangerous taverns; those who received a taste of "mountain justice" after a woman's honor was besmirched; and the Muncie cop cut down in a senseless killing.

Muncie had the best and worst to offer, from the police officers who roamed and robbed, to the officers who spent years tracking down the killer of a lonely woman.

Muncie, Indiana, is the stuff of legends, of heroes and villains, of murder and mayhem.

# 1.

# THE CITY EVERYONE SHUNNED

In 1893, Lizzie Borden was found not guilty of murdering her parents in Massachusetts. Also that year, the *Indiana*, the first battleship of its kind in the U.S. Navy, was launched. Arthur Conan Doyle killed off his creation, Sherlock Holmes, at the hands of villainous James Moriarty in "The Final Problem."

In Muncie, a city not yet thirty years old and experiencing growing pains, Dr. Frank Jackson had an alarming problem.

Jackson had been named the city's first health officer, a position for which he was paid $400 a year. At thirty-four, he was a young physician compared to others in Muncie. He was bucking his elders, then, when he suggested that the cases of chickenpox the city was seeing were not chickenpox. The illness was smallpox, and it was deadly.

Not that Jackson could convince some people of his diagnosis—at least not at first. Before Muncie's smallpox epidemic of 1893 was beaten back, reputations were won and lost, an entire portion of the city was quarantined and neighbors spread the disease not only through ignorance and arrogance but also malice.

Muncie and Delaware County were undergoing a boom just as smallpox broke out. It wasn't the first time smallpox was found in the city, and it wouldn't be the last, but the epidemic of 1893 was notable because of its virulence and because of how the city reacted.

In 1893, Muncie was growing. Many of its twenty-two thousand residents had come from the southern United States, looking for work. They were

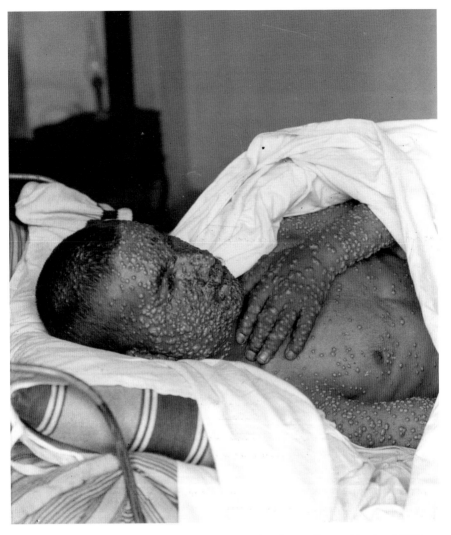

A smallpox patient like those in Muncie, Indiana, during the smallpox epidemic of 1893. *Library of Congress.*

the first wave of people looking to make their fortune—or at least a good living—in Muncie. The discovery of natural gas in the Midwest in the 1880s brought speculators and developers, would-be industrialists and the workers they needed.

The Ball Brothers, container makers from New York, were searching Ohio in 1886 for a possible factory site when a Muncie businessman contacted them and offered to show them around the town. By 1888, the Ball Brothers were settled in Muncie after accepting incentives that included $7,500, free land for their factory, a railroad siding and a supply of natural gas, free of charge, for five years. By 1893, the Balls were making nine million home food canning jars a year in Muncie.

Although the Balls' manufacturing dominance—and influence—in Muncie would last for decades, the natural gas supply did not. Natural gas wells were left to burn around the clock because the powers that be believed that gas would last for seven hundred years. It did not. By the early 1900s, the natural gas supply was exhausted.

But in 1893, the city was riding high on the seemingly inexhaustible supply of fuel and the workers attracted by the city's burgeoning industry. With them came their children: Muncie's schools, which had begun in the city even before the city was incorporated, had several thousand students by 1893. The first high school had opened in 1881, and in 1893, Blaine School, the latest of several school buildings, opened.

The children of Muncie, unfortunately, were the easiest targets of smallpox.

It was August 1893, and the Delaware County Fair, an annual event that draws the town's residents to this day, was underway. According to William G. Eidson's 1990 article "Confusion, Controversy and Quarantine: The Muncie Smallpox Epidemic of 1893," as many as ten thousand fairgoers—nearly half the city—were enjoying horse races and hot-air balloons.

Instead of enjoying the fair, Doctor Jackson was making a house call at the Macedonia Avenue home of Thomas Murray and his family. Dr. Robert Bunch, whose son Rollin would later be mayor of Muncie, had diagnosed the Murray family with chickenpox.

Jackson doubted the diagnosis of the forty-one-year-old, well-established Bunch, however, and was worried that the high fever and skin eruptions were symptoms of smallpox, not chickenpox. Jackson contacted the Indiana State Board of Health, and Dr. Charles Metcalf came to Muncie and confirmed that the illness was smallpox.

Jackson quickly met with members of Muncie City Council and convinced several of the officials that smallpox was not only present in the city but also spreading. The disease had been introduced in April when a visitor from New Jersey, infected with smallpox, visited a local family, the Dilks, who then passed the disease to the Malloy family. One of the Malloy children went to class at Blaine, where she sat next to a child from the Murray family. The Malloy girl had smallpox blisters on her face but still went to school.

A classroom at Blaine Elementary School in Muncie in the late 1800s. Smallpox spread among children at the school in 1893. *Ball State University Digital Archives.*

The Murray girl had been treated by Dr. Bunch in May, while school was still in session, but her illness was diagnosed as chickenpox.

Throughout the summer, Dr. Bunch saw and treated patients with smallpox—but he diagnosed them with chickenpox despite severe blistering, high fevers and convulsions. Bunch decided to notify Jackson and the health department in August, although he still maintained that the sick were afflicted with chickenpox.

At Jackson's urging in mid-August, city officials approved quarantines of houses where smallpox had been diagnosed. Yellow cardboard signs reading "smallpox" were posted on the houses and, Eidson wrote, guards were stationed near the houses to prevent coming and going.

All but one of the families lived near a wooded area that would come to be known as Heekin Park, in a portion of the city that was eight blocks wide and sixteen blocks long. In an area bounded by Willard Street, Macedonia Avenue, Walnut Street and Ohmer Avenue (later renamed Twelfth Street and, still later, Memorial Drive), red warning flags were erected, but entry and exit from the area was not prohibited. Only comings and goings from the individual houses were forbidden.

Groceries, milk and even water were delivered at a safe distance. Doctors entering each infected house wore rubber coats and boots. Eventually, even the guards watching the borders of the area were required to spend their off-hours there. Eidson wrote that two people were arrested for breaking quarantine, although they were not the only violators.

The city quickly began vaccinating Muncie residents. If people couldn't afford the fifty-cent cost of the shot, the city would pay for it.

Even while precautions were being taken, a group of smallpox disbelievers arose. Among the most prominent among them was Dr. Bunch, who continued to say publicly that the disease was chickenpox, not smallpox.

For a few days, no new cases were reported. That late August break in the disease's spread caused many to join Bunch in doubting that smallpox was among them. The quarantine was still on, however. With guards out front, members of infected families left by their houses' back doors, traveling throughout the city. Garbage men refused to collect the trash from infected houses, and it piled up outside rather than being burned.

The Delaware County health officer, Hugh Cowing, said that he and his city counterpart Jackson and other authorities had to fight not only the disease but also "the surroundings and the people" of Muncie.

Mayor Arthur Brady brought Indianapolis physician Henry Jamison to town, and Jamison argued that the epidemic would get worse if a smallpox hospital, or "pest house," was not created. But city officials said they wouldn't open a smallpox hospital, because so many people in Muncie didn't believe the disease was present. Officials cited 1885 riots in Montreal when that Canadian city tried to force smallpox patients into pest houses.

The debate continued. Then, all hell broke loose.

As Eidson wrote, in late August and early September, "dozens" of new smallpox cases in Muncie were identified. A sixteen-year-old girl, Mary Emma Russell, died. And cases of smallpox were found outside the quarantine zone.

On September 7, the state board of health did what Muncie officials wouldn't do: impose a restrictive quarantine on the city. Public gatherings, whether at churches, ball games or schools, were outlawed. The public wasn't allowed to gather on the street, and police could make arrests for "loitering or loafing." And thousands were to be vaccinated. In fact, the entire population was subject to vaccination orders.

The Delaware County commissioners followed suit and shut down church services and schools, including those that were yet to begin classes for the fall. Spurious smallpox "cure" recipes were printed in local newspapers.

The state told people outside Muncie that they entered the city at their own risk. Those who wanted to leave the city by train had to be certified healthy by authorities, and other cities hired police officers to ensure that people from Muncie had that certification before crossing their borders. Neighboring Randolph County said that visitors from Muncie would be quarantined for ten days. The baggage of travelers from Muncie had to be fumigated before it left the city. Even letters and packages were fumigated by the post office, and library books returned from the quarantine area were burned. Panic broke out in the town of Daleville when a man told people he had a visitor from Muncie who might be infected. The visitor, a boy, was found as he fished, but physicians determined the rash on his body was from poison ivy, not smallpox.

Mothers in Anderson reportedly told their children that if they didn't go to bed, they would be punished by being sent to Muncie.

The smallpox plague finally had the public's attention.

Officials quickly moved to build a pest house in the woods in what would later be called Heekin Park. Patients were reluctant to leave their homes, and authorities enacted plans to have them forcibly removed.

As an initial measure, however, health officials urged friends of smallpox-infected families to persuade the sick to go to the hospital. One family threw rocks at a friend who implored them to go. In another incident, a father shot and wounded a man who tried to take his sick child to the hospital. One family refused to go, and officials decided to cut off their food supply to force them out of their home, but friends sneaked food in to them. In one instance, a man threatened officials with a gun rather than give up his sick father, who died a few days later.

While authorities worked to open a second hospital and persuade the sick to commit themselves for treatment, some from smallpox houses took infected rags and threw them at the houses of people who were not infected in an attempt to spread the disease.

Ignorance wasn't limited to the general public. Dr. Bunch and other Muncie physicians joined the Indiana Anti-Vaccination Society and continued to maintain that chickenpox, not deadly smallpox, infected Muncie. Some of those smallpox deniers issued proof-of-vaccination paperwork to their patients who were, in reality, not vaccinated.

The debate ended up in court, where a judge said health officials could mandate vaccinations. So ten thousand Muncie residents were given preventative shots.

Successive waves of the disease hit Muncie, with more than one hundred infected by October. But as fall passed into winter, the progress of the disease slowed. Nevertheless, Eidson wrote, twenty-two people died during the Muncie smallpox epidemic of 1893. No funerals were allowed, however, and all of the victims were buried in the middle of the night.

Fighting smallpox cost the city $22,807, and Indiana's governor, Claude Matthews, considered financial help for the city. But some smallpox deniers from Muncie wrote to the governor to argue that state money shouldn't go to the city, which, the writers maintained, had blown the epidemic out of proportion.

By November, with the likelihood that the epidemic had subsided, the quarantine was lifted; schools opened for the year and churches and organizations held their first public gatherings in weeks.

The ripples from the smallpox epidemic of 1893 were felt for decades to come. In 1913, county health commissioner Hugh Cowing said that he considered smallpox a continuing threat. In 1932, now retired Cowing recalled for the *Muncie Evening Press* the middle-of-the-night burials of smallpox victims of the 1893 epidemic. In 1937, Mayor Rollin Bunch—son of the smallpox denier of 1893 and a physician himself—recommended vaccinations as a mini-outbreak of smallpox occurred. Five cases were under quarantine. Another handful of smallpox cases was diagnosed in 1938.

In 1943, on the fiftieth anniversary of the epidemic, Cowing noted that severe blows were dealt to the city by the epidemic. "The epidemic taxed the doctors, health officials and nurses beyond capacity," Cowing wrote in the *Muncie Star*. "For weeks, Muncie was quarantined from the outside world....After fifty years, the lesson of this epidemic remains: Vaccinate and prevent smallpox."

It was not until 1979 that smallpox was declared eradicated throughout the world.

And in Muncie.

# 2.
# JULES LADURON'S EARLY YEARS

Jules LaDuron had a talent for making the news. He did it often throughout the twentieth century, sometimes for his political accomplishments, sometimes for his medical career—and sometimes for the sudden death or disappearance of those in his life.

For a man whose life was in the headlines over the course of seven decades, it's not surprising that Jules LaDuron—athlete, politician, family man and physician—became one of the best-known and, at times, most controversial figures in Muncie in the twentieth century.

LaDuron's penchant for appearing in the headlines started early. He was only a sophomore at Muncie High School in May 1911 when, in what was likely the first of many times his name appeared in newspapers, he broke a fellow student's jaw with a roundhouse punch. On page nine of the *Muncie Morning Star* on May 18, 1911, an article headlined "Students in a Fight; One Gets a Broken Jaw," recapped an incident among high school students during a baseball game at McCulloch Park the previous day. "Class spirit reached so high a pitch that a clash ensued between some of the students and in the mix-up, Russell Beck, a junior, had two teeth knocked out and his jaw broken."

Near the end of the game, the article reported, an argument broke out among students watching the game and "Jules LaDuron, a sophomore, took exception to some of the remarks and with a heavy right he swung into a crowd of juniors standing behind him."

Young Jules LaDuron. *LaDuron family.*

"The blow struck Beck squarely on the jaw and had he not been standing in a crowd he probably would have gone down for the count of ten," the article continued. "He was taken to the office of Dr. Owens where it was found his jaw was broken. As a result of the mix-up, charges may be filed by some of the students."

On May 18, Delaware County court records show, an arrest warrant was issued for LaDuron for assault and battery. The case was ultimately dismissed for lack of sufficient evidence.

It wasn't unheard of for incidents and grievances that might be considered a small matter to be fodder for newspapers. In an article next to the one-paragraph LaDuron story was one in which an Albany woman was reported to have sued for divorce, maintaining that her husband had left her three years earlier for another woman.

A little more than a year after LaDuron's brush with the law, he was chosen by fellow students to represent them on a board with the aim of "reviving" Muncie High School athletics. The school had been "a terror" in football in 1905 and 1906 but had been on a "downward path" in the years since, according to newspaper accounts. One hurdle LaDuron and his fellow committee members had to overcome: convincing the school corporation to build a gym.

LaDuron's physicality played into his post–high school years in ways both good and bad. His oldest grandson and namesake, Jules, recalled in a fall 2017 interview that his grandfather was well over six feet tall and a natural athlete. The elder LaDuron was a friend of Jim Thorpe, the Native American athlete who won gold medals in the 1912 Olympics, family members say. LaDuron was considered as a competitor in the hammer throw but ended up instead accompanying Thorpe and taking care of the medalist's pit bulls.

BORN IN 1893—THE YEAR of the Muncie smallpox epidemic—Jules LaDuron was the son of Fernando Jules LaDuron, a native of Belgium, and Jemima

Joris, from Norristown, Pennsylvania. The couple also raised a daughter, Grace Adele, who was a Muncie schoolteacher for thirty years before retiring to Florida.

Jules LaDuron was rarely out of the headlines for most of his life. In 1914, newspapers recounted how the "big high school athlete" would likely play varsity football at Indiana University. In August 1914, LaDuron was attending IU classes at Winona Lake when he disappeared. Fernando told reporters that his son had left school and was on his way to New York, where he hoped to join the Belgian army and fight in the European war. Jules LaDuron had reportedly spoken "enthusiastically" about the war.

"The young man had been seen talking to strange men at Winona," and the older LaDuron believed the men were agents of Belgium or France, recruiting the brawny young man for service. Fernando LaDuron had come from Belgium to Muncie to open a factory for blown-glass products.

Jules LaDuron, at age twenty, returned to Indiana a few days after disappearing without successfully enlisting, although some records

Newspaper clipping of photo of the Congerville Flyers in 1910, including Jules LaDuron (*second row, left*). *LaDuron family.*

from late in LaDuron's life indicate that he did serve in the U.S. Army Ambulance Corps.

LaDuron had a brief run with the Congerville (sometimes Muncie) Flyers, a fledgling NFL team that played for about twenty years until 1926. By October 1921, LaDuron had joined the Flyers. A newspaper account noted that the Flyers were "expected to wade through the ranks of the American Professional Football Association," later known as the National Football League. LaDuron, who had by that time studied medicine at the University of Kentucky, had played football at the school in the fullback position. He had graduated from the medical school at the University of Kentucky in June 1920.

Not all the stories about LaDuron were in the sports section of the newspaper. In August 1925, LaDuron was arrested on assault charges after Kathleen Armint told police that LaDuron, by now a practicing physician, pushed her down a flight of stairs at his downtown Muncie office. LaDuron said Armint had attempted to strike him and fell down the stairs. In early 1926, a Henry County jury found him not guilty of another assault charge in connection with battering a New Castle taxi driver, George Baughn. After a city court conviction, the case was reversed at the county court level. The taxi driver testified that he couldn't accurately identify LaDuron because

Photo of Jules LaDuron in football gear in 1913. *LaDuron family.*

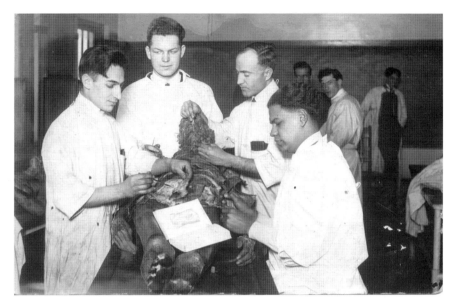

Jules LaDuron, at head of the autopsy table, and fellow University of Kentucky students examine a cadaver. *LaDuron family.*

he had been asleep when his assailant became enraged after Baughn didn't immediately respond to a request to fix a tire.

LaDuron's exposure to death and suffering came early. According to 1972 court documents, while he was attending medical school in Louisville, he was called into service during the influenza pandemic of 1918 that saw between fifty million and one hundred million people die worldwide.

As a medical student, LaDuron was called to Camp Taylor outside Louisville to help treat flu patients there. He transported bodies to the morgue and patients to hospitals. It was common for a dozen people to die every day, LaDuron recalled years later. It was "only by the grace of God" that he didn't contract the deadly flu as he carried, often in his arms, flu patients to ambulances for transport to hospitals.

In 1927, LaDuron's life was first hit by the kind of unexpected tragedy that would eventually become a hallmark. That spring, LaDuron had married Edna Duerr, a resident of Louisville, Kentucky. Six weeks after the wedding, in June, Edna LaDuron hanged herself in the attic of her mother's home in Louisville. Edna's mother found her daughter's body.

Edna had been in Muncie just a few days before her suicide, newspapers noted, although she had spent three weeks at her mother's house to recover from a "nervous collapse." No suicide note was left, but authorities believed

Edna had killed herself due to "ill health." In 1972 court documents, her illness was identified as cancer.

In the weeks following the tragedy, the *Muncie Morning Star*'s "society" page reported in late July that LaDuron and his sister, Adele, had traveled to Cheyenne, Wyoming, to attend a rodeo and then journey to Yellowstone National Park.

The Yellowstone trip was a relatively modest one for LaDuron, his grandson said decades later. LaDuron was a world traveler, visiting Mexico and Canada as well as countries in Europe and South America. He spoke several languages "fluently" and practiced orthopedic medicine in Belgium after earning his medical degree. For a period of time, he practiced medicine in Virginia, traveling on horseback to treat patients.

Some of Jules LaDuron's fame had to do with his political activity. Newspaper accounts reflect that LaDuron ran for Delaware County coroner in 1928. Perhaps the plunge into politics was something that the physician had always wanted to try, or perhaps he wanted to change his life following Edna's sudden death.

LaDuron was operating his own medical office—two of them, as a matter of fact, at 2020 East Willard Street in the morning and at 112 West Adams Street in the afternoon and as late as 9:00 in the evening—in 1928, when he was notably active in government and politics.

In the May 1928 primary—an election in which Herbert Hoover swept Delaware County's voters—LaDuron sought the Democratic Party nomination for county coroner. When the ballots were counted, however, physician Arnold Tucker apparently defeated LaDuron by a single vote. That outcome changed when the ballots from the last of the county's forty-two political precincts were counted: The contest for the Democratic Party nomination was tied.

A recount by party officials put LaDuron over the top; he was the Democratic Party nominee in the November 1928 election. But the spring victory only set him up for disappointment in the fall, when political novice Clarence Piepho defeated LaDuron "in a top-heavy majority of over 6,500 votes."

Despite his foray into politics, LaDuron didn't ignore his medical practice. An article from a month before his political candidacy noted that his East Willard Street office, dubbed a "hospital," had wards and private rooms and an X-ray machine.

LaDuron continued to move in the top political circles in Muncie. In January 1929, the Delaware County commissioners named LaDuron chief physician for both the county infirmary and county jail. In 1932, LaDuron and fellow physician Rollin H. Bunch—who had been Muncie's mayor until 1919, when he was convicted of mail fraud and sentenced to two years in prison, only to win a pardon from President Woodrow Wilson—were present, presumably to offer medical aid, at a boxing match at the National Guard Armory.

The association with Bunch benefited LaDuron two years later, when Bunch, despite the scandal of his earlier time in office, was elected mayor in 1934. Even before he took office, Bunch let it be known that LaDuron had a spot in his administration. According to a December 1934 article in the *Muncie Evening Press*, Bunch said he would name LaDuron city health commissioner.

By the end of December, Bunch had made the appointment and LaDuron—who at this point had a medical office at 519 South Liberty Street—saw his photo in newspapers for a happier circumstance than would follow in just a few years.

LaDuron was paid $6,845 for his job as health commissioner in 1935. It was, according to newspaper accounts, twice the budget for the health department.

As the city's top health officer, LaDuron approved the hiring of two men from Tampa, Florida, to pursue a citywide program of extermination of vermin—rats, ants, termites and roaches. Perhaps because he was born the year of the smallpox outbreak, he was conscious of the community's public health needs.

Jules LaDuron wasn't alone in celebrating his political fortunes. By the time he won his prominent position, he had remarried. The manner in which that marriage ended cast a shadow over Jules LaDuron and his family for decades.

## 3.

# WAITING FOR HARRY BATEMAN

T here are several people buried in Muncie's Beech Grove Cemetery whose identities presumably will never be known.

Among them are a man, woman and child—likely buried a century or so earlier—whose remains were found when a basement was being dug in the 300 block of East Wysor Street in March 1948. The bones of a few early Muncie settlers were uncovered in 1907, when work was being done at the current site of Friends Memorial Church, 418 West Adams Street. Those remains were re-interred at Beech Grove.

The bodies of at least two men found floating in White River, one in 1965 and the other fifty-eight years earlier, are among the cemetery's nameless population. So, too, is a man who was buried in March 1889 after his dismembered remains were recovered from along the Bee Line railroad tracks west of Muncie. Authorities of his day were at least certain of what that man's name was not—Harry F. Bateman.

When the man's body was found—its head, legs and an arm severed as a result of contact with the train, according to the *Free Press* of Burlington, Vermont—the initial assumption was that the remains were those of Bateman.

The resident of Fostoria, Ohio—about 150 miles northeast of Delaware County—had been seen in Muncie a day earlier, when he rented a horse and buggy at a local livery stable, indicating that he intended to take a ride "into the country."

About 2:20 a.m. the following day, the horse returned to the stable, pulling a buggy that was unoccupied. Forty minutes after the horse arrived at the stable, the westbound train about two miles away struck and shredded the body. On its torso was found a "light-colored overcoat" that appeared identical to that worn by Bateman the previous day.

In a pocket was a $5,000 life insurance policy, taken out in Bateman's name with the U.S. Accident Insurance Company of Brooklyn, New York. Also found in the coat were a letter, bearing Bateman's signature, on stationery from the French Hotel of Lima, Ohio, and a note asking that the U.S. Army be notified in the event of Bateman's death.

In an apparent coincidence, Parker Bugsley, Bateman's brother-in-law, was a railroad employee on the train when the body was struck. Later given an opportunity to examine the remains, he insisted they were not those of Bateman.

Over the next two days, Bateman's wife, sister and John Quincy Adams Campbell, editor of the *Bellefontaine (Ohio) Republican*, traveled to Muncie and declared "positively the remains are not those of Harry F. Bateman," the *Indianapolis Journal* reported.

The would-be widow did acknowledge that the coat and documents were her husband's, however. She said her husband had intended to travel to Anderson to discuss the possibility of locating a glass plant there. She had

A horse-drawn hearse from Muncie in the late 1800s. *Ball State University Digital Archives.*

also received a letter from her husband mailed from Muncie the day before the body was discovered.

A coroner reported that a bruise on the severed skull's forehead led him to suspect the man had been struck with a blunt object before being left on the tracks. During an autopsy, the victim's stomach was removed "to be sent to a chemist," the *Journal* reported. "There are a thousand theories, and it is very hard to tell the correct one," the Indianapolis newspaper concluded.

With growing suspicion that the man struck by the train had been murdered, perhaps by Bateman, accounts of the mystery appeared in newspapers throughout the nation. The *Los Angeles Times* declared it a "diabolical crime" and suggested the victim had been slain "presumably to swindle insurance companies."

It was determined that Bateman was a lieutenant in the U.S. Army, assigned to a cavalry regiment based in Kansas. He had deserted, perhaps after allegations of financial improprieties with payroll money were raised. He had also for a time gone by another name.

War Department officials, when informed of Batemen's possible death, assumed at first that he had committed suicide, the *Los Angeles Herald* reported.

Back in Muncie, hundreds of curious residents were reported to have filed past the victim's remains. "The affair has created intense excitement," the *Manhattan (Kansas) Mercury* reported, "and the entire community has resolved itself into a detective association."

The *Journal* published a detailed description of the unknown man: "about 5 feet 7 inches tall, light complexion, black hair, hazel eyes, thin, light mustached, about 35." His socks were "marked with an 'H,'" it was noted. Mrs. Bateman had observed that the victim's hands were rough—suggesting he was a "farmer or a plasterer," the *Journal* said—while her husband's were "smooth and soft."

Speculation on the body's identity focused for a time on John Eastman, reported to be missing from his Pendleton home. (Eastman surfaced unharmed but, incredibly, was killed in September 1890 when a wagon he was a passenger in was struck by a train at a Bee Line crossing southwest of Anderson.)

Claims that the Muncie body might be that of Albert Parmenter—like Bateman, a resident of Fostoria—were dismissed after the Ohio man came forward to declare he was alive and well.

A few days later, the Muncie Police Department received a letter—from Harry F. Bateman, of all people. In the letter—dated two days after the body's discovery and mailed in Terre Haute—Bateman said he was startled to read in a newspaper that he was presumed to have been killed in Delaware County. "That it was not my body, I am well able to demonstrate," he wrote.

He told a tale of being approached by a "hard-looking man" down on his luck while in Muncie. "I took pity on the poor devil," Bateman wrote, saying he had bought the man a meal, and after hearing his tale of misfortune, was moved to give him his overcoat. It was only later, Bateman said, that he was chagrined to realize he had left documents and letters in that coat.

That evening, Bateman recounted, he hastily boarded a train bound for Indianapolis and gave his new friend three dollars to return the rented horse and buggy to the stable. "He said his name was Neal, I think," the Ohio man wrote. "I took quite an interest in the man, and felt he was honest….I have no theory to advance at to the cause of his death—if it is he."

Bateman said he was en route to Colorado but would return in about two weeks and will "stop in Muncie and see you." He concluded that he was "hoping to hear that you have succeeded in unraveling the mystery as to the cause of the poor fellow's death."

"Muncie people don't believe the story, and Bateman will be arrested," the *Daily Monitor* in Fort Scott, Kansas, reported. Actually, that was half right.

Few people in Muncie believed Bateman's account of his dealings while in Delaware County, or that he wasn't somehow responsible for the stranger's death on the railroad tracks. And few were likely surprised when, his assertions in his letter aside, Bateman never showed up in Muncie and was not heard from again.

Nearly 130 years later, the mystery remains unsolved.

# 4.
# MOUNTAIN JUSTICE

On his first—and perhaps only—trip to Muncie, twenty-six-year-old Vaughn Yates of Bone Cave, Tennessee, shot a man to death, seemingly in cold blood.

For his efforts, Yates appeared for a time to achieve the status of a folk hero, at least among a segment of east central Indiana's population.

On the evening of Sunday, November 21, 1937, Ezra Cole and his bride, Virginia—more commonly known as "Virgie"—had just arrived at their home, an apartment house in the 1000 block of North Blaine Street, when a gunman emerged from the darkness. As the man moved closer, Virgie recognized him as her brother, Vaughn.

The Coles had moved to Muncie a few months earlier from Bone Cave, a tiny hamlet in the hills of Tennessee's Van Buren County, about halfway between Nashville and Knoxville. Ezra, thirty-two, was employed on a local Works Progress Administration project.

Conflicting accounts would be given about Ezra Cole's interactions, over the course of the next few seconds, with his gun-toting brother-in-law. The gun—later described as a "cheap, long-barrel .32-caliber revolver"—was fired once, in Cole's direction, producing no immediate reaction from its target. "Vaughn, don't do that!" Virgie screamed at her brother. A second shot tore into Ezra Cole's stomach. He collapsed against a nearby car. His wife fainted.

At that point—according to eyewitness Clarence Steakley, a cousin to Virgie and Vaughn who lived in Muncie with the Coles—Vaughn Yates

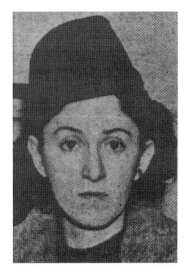

Virgie Yates, the woman whose virtue was worth killing over for her brother. *Muncie Newspapers.*

stood over his swooning sister, pointed his firearm at Virgie and pulled the trigger three or four times. The gun didn't discharge, however.

Yates then returned to the taxi cab that had brought him to the Cole home and left the scene. "Well, that's over," he said to cab driver Donald Say. The shooting victim was raced to Ball Memorial Hospital, where he would linger, in critical condition, for four days.

According to Say, Yates told him to stop in an alley near Mulberry and Seventh Streets, where he buried his gun in a snowdrift. Vaughn Yates then went to the local bus station but learned the next bus bound for Indianapolis wouldn't leave until 3:00 a.m. Instead, he checked in at the downtown Dearmin Hotel, at Seymour and Walnut Streets, identifying himself as "John Westbrook of Cincinnati."

He was apprehended in his room that night, without incident, by three city police detectives. The Tennessean then gave them his reasons for shooting Cole. His explanation would result in national news coverage.

According to Yates, after working for nearly three years at Civilian Conservation Corps camps in the Appalachians—and sending nearly all of his income home to Bone Cave to help support his family—he had found a job at a paper mill in Kingsport, Tennessee.

Then came word from Vaughn's father. Virgie had run off to Indiana with Ezra Cole, he said, and the elder Yates could find no indication in area clerk's offices that the two had married. "When my father and I could find no record of the marriage, I got a .32-caliber revolver and came to Muncie, by bus and train," Vaughn told police. The purpose of the four-hundred-mile trip was "to get the man that stole my sister away from her home," he said, explaining it "was not the only dishonor [Cole] had heaped upon us."

Yates said that about five years earlier, Cole had impregnated his other sister then failed to either marry her or help provide for their child. The son she gave birth to added to "the folk I had to help feed with my camp income," Vaughn said. "I didn't want my other sister to be mistreated."

According to Muncie police detective Harry Massey, Vaughn Yates told him, "If they were married, I'm sorry. If they weren't, I can't see that I did anything wrong."

Virgie and her cousin Steakley were also detained in the Delaware County jail to ensure their availability to testify, first before a grand jury and then, presumably, at trial. (She was allowed to visit the shooting victim in his hospital room.)

For her part, the twenty-nine-year-old Virgie maintained that she believed she had married Cole during a May 8 trip to a clerk's office in Woodbury, Tennessee, about forty miles west of Bone Cave. She acknowledged that she hadn't been asked to sign any papers that day.

Local news stories described Vaughn Yates as "the black-haired, cold-eyed son of Bone Cave, Tenn….born of the clan spirit of the Tennessee hill country."

Headlines across the country referred to Yates's pursuit of "mountain justice" and an "honor shooting." By week's end, that would change to an "honor killing."

At 6:20 a.m. on Thursday, November 25—Thanksgiving—Ezra Cole died. His body would be returned to his native Van Buren County for burial. ("Son, brother, how we miss you," his tombstone read.) Later that day, reporters were allowed to look on as Vaughn was led to Virgie's cell in the county jail. The siblings, the iron bars between them, sobbed as they spoke.

"Virgie, how are you?" Vaughn asked his sister.

"Don't you worry about me," she responded.

"But you are the greatest worry I got," Vaughn told her.

"Ezra didn't want you prosecuted for this," Virgie said. "He told me at the hospital before he died."

Virgie also said the dying man had also confessed to her that, strictly speaking, they weren't legally married. "I'm sorry this had to happen this way," her brother responded. "I really am."

A few days later, a local grand jury indicted Yates on charges of first- and second-degree murder. Later, prosecutor Clarence G. "Mike" Higi said he did not intend to seek a death sentence in the case, which was moved in January to Randolph County due to pretrial publicity.

As the trial, set for March 1938, approached, *Muncie Evening Press* editor Wilbur Sutton wrote that he was looking forward to the coverage. "Long time since Muncie has had a murder trial with the human interest that of Vaughn Yates promises to be," he wrote. "Several of the necessary elements there—love, hate, honor of the family, good-looking girl and even the

"Mountain Justice" Sends Man to Jail as His Victim Fights for Life at the Hospital

Believing that his sister, Virginia, 28, was living in adultery with Ezra Cole, 30, Vaughn Yates, 26, of Bone Cave, Tenn., bought a pistol, hurried to Muncie and shot Cole through the stomach late yesterday. Cole and the woman contend they were married in Tennessee before coming to Muncie. Yates is pictured above, with Lt. Det. August Feltz, left, and Det. E. B. Ransdell, right. He is being held in jail while Cole is near death at Ball Hospital. Mrs. Cole is shown below.

Newspaper clipping of Vaughn Yates (*center*) with authorities after his arrest. *Muncie Newspapers.*

picturesqueness associated with Tennessee mountaineers. Only drawback is that those involved are not socially prominent or wealthy."

The trial began on March 14, two days after Vaughn Yates had observed his twenty-seventh birthday in the Randolph County jail in Winchester. Among the witnesses called to the stand was the defendant's sixty-three-year-old father, Luther Clint Yates, a tenant farmer who had lived in Bone Cave all of his life. He recalled the fateful evening he came home for dinner and found a note, from his daughter Virgie, on his dresser. "She [wrote] she had left with Ezra Cole," the father told the jury.

Later, the elder Yates met with reporters and said he had never been "north" before. "I haven't had much time to look around, but the people are mighty nice," he said.

As he waited to take the stand on March 16, Vaughn Yates sat in the courthouse's law library with Randolph County sheriff Lester Mann and looked out a window at the horizon. "Mighty level here," he told the sheriff. "I'm anxious to see any hills."

When called to testify, Yates maintained that he had fired his gun in self-defense, now claiming that Cole had pulled a knife on him. "My intention was to ask Cole if he had a legal right to live with my sister," Yates said. "He didn't seem to want to settle it that way. I didn't intend to hurt him or anyone else. When I pulled the trigger a second time, he kind of fell back and hollered he was shot."

During his cross-examination of the defendant, Higi suggested that the comparative metropolis of Muncie "must have seemed pretty big" to the Tennessean. "You've been living down there in Bone Cave," Higi said. "Just a grocery store, I suppose."

"I don't think there's even a grocery store there!" Yates exclaimed.

In his closing remarks, on March 17, defense attorney Clarence Benadum compared his client to the Messiah. "There were times in the life of Jesus Christ when he believed it was proper to carry a weapon," Benadum said, adding that Yates came to Muncie knowing he would "meet in battle…to protect the honor of his sister."

"When a man takes a girl away from home for the purpose Ezra Cole did," Benadum told jurors, "he is worse, if you please, than the man who blows a hole in a bank safe and takes somebody's money.

"I think this jury ought to vote [Yates's] expenses back to Tennessee."

Yates's other defense attorney, Van Ogle, urged jurors to consider that "the community in which these persons live is almost removed from society.…There was some sort of mock ceremony, but there was no record of any marriage."

An emotional Higi raised his voice when he addressed jurors. "We want him to know he can't come to Delaware County and kill a man and then go free to the sidewalks," the prosecutor said.

"This man had a six-inch pistol when he left the state of Tennessee and he thought so much of it that he carried it in his belt. He didn't put it in his suitcase. He didn't intend to visit his sister. He intended only to kill Cole and return to the hills of his native state."

The jury deliberated for five hours and forty-five minutes that afternoon and evening before returning a not-guilty verdict about 9:00 p.m. Judge Alonzo L. Bales rapped his gavel for order in the courtroom after the announcement of the verdict prompted spectators to begin to cheer. However, the *Evening Press* reported, exuberant spectators "surged forward to shake the hand of Yates, the same hand which pulled a trigger." According to the *Press*, "Yates and his elderly father rushed to the jurors and shook hands with the 10 men and two women who exonerated the defendant. And the quiet town of Winchester celebrated." (Members of the jury would later contribute to a fund to help pay for Vaughn Yates's trip home to Tennessee.) A *Muncie Star* headline the next morning proclaimed that "mountain justice" had been upheld by the jurors.

Later that day, *Evening Press* editor Sutton had harsh words for the Randolph County jury. "One thing that Winchester jury failed to do—decorate with a gold medal the breast of Vaughn Yates, who armed himself at his home in Tennessee, deliberately journeyed to Muncie and here killed at night the man who ran away with his sister," Sutton wrote.

"A sister who, apparently, is past the age of a minor and presumably capable of knowing what she was doing. A good many years ago, when

Delaware County juries had established a reputation for freeing murderers, it was a common saying in other parts of the state, 'I'll take you over to Muncie and kill you.'

"Apparently Randolph County jurors are of the same makeup."

Immediately after his acquittal in the murder case, Yates was arrested again, accused of carrying a pistol without a permit on the night of Cole's shooting. He was returned to Muncie and the Delaware County jail.

Benadum was outraged by his client's second arrest, accusing Higi of "vicious conduct in official office." The gun case would not proceed, however. A week after Yates's acquittal in the murder case, Higi dismissed the weapons charge, writing in a motion that he believed there was "insufficient evidence to obtain a conviction in this cause." The prosecutor had reportedly been unable to find a city police officer willing to sign a probable cause affidavit in the gun case.

And police chief Frank Massey noted that former residents of Tennessee and Kentucky now living in Muncie were circulating petitions calling for Yates's freedom. "I think I be goin' back to Tennessee," Yates said as he was released from the jail on May 23, 123 days after arriving in Muncie.

The *Evening Press* reported that Yates was wistful about leaving behind the handgun he had used to kill Cole, which remained in police custody.

Local authorities heard of Vaughn Yates only once more, in January 1942. Police in Memphis contacted their Muncie counterparts and reported that Yates was in custody there. They didn't say what had led to Yates's Memphis arrest but did inquire whether the murder charge lodged against him in Muncie more than four years earlier was still pending.

The Tennessee authorities were assured that Yates had been given a "clean bill" when it came to the Delaware County allegations.

Virgie Yates did not return to Bone Cave with her brother. She married a local man, had two children and lived in the Yorktown area for several years. She did return to Tennessee when the marriage ended in the late 1950s but settled in Nashville, not Bone Cave.

That's where she was living when her brother Vaughn—by then a resident of Lebanon, Tennessee, about sixty miles from his hometown—died at age fifty-nine in February 1971. Virgie lived into her nineties, by one account passing away two days after the start of the new millennium, in January 2000.

# 5.

# GEORGE DALE VS. THE KKK

There are few men in Muncie's history as controversial—hailed as a hero by many, hated by others—as George R. Dale, former mayor and newspaper publisher.

And there are few fights in Muncie history as riveting and as odd as Dale's fight against the Ku Klux Klan.

When Dale died at his home on March 27, 1936, the *Muncie Evening Press* hailed him as a "vigorous crusader," which he certainly was. But the fact that one of the city's two longtime establishment newspapers said so, considering that Dale had published an independent newspaper that frequently criticized not only the KKK and the political establishment but also news coverage of both, was interesting.

"Dale lived through stormy days and years when the Klan was in its heyday," the obituary noted. "Years that took him time and time again into court on charges of being in contempt or of libel.

"His adventures in those days before he became Muncie's mayor would have filled a book—a volume that Dale often thought of writing but never really got around to doing."

To understand Dale, his life and his high-profile battle with the Klan, which included two incidents that Dale maintained were attempts on his life but that some skeptics later doubted, it's good to have an understanding of the activities of the Ku Klux Klan in Muncie and in the rest of Indiana.

Dwight W. Hoover's 1986 book about Muncie, *Magic Middletown*, contains a chapter, "The Klan in Muncie," that features photographer W. Arthur

A rally of the Muncie chapter of the Ku Klux Klan in 1922. *Ball State University Digital Archives.*

Swift's startling photos of hooded and robed KKK members gathering in Muncie. Swift's photos and Hoover's text paint a fascinating picture of the Klan in the small American city that had been portrayed in Robert and Helen Lynds's sociological study "Middletown" as typical.

Hoover writes that the modern-day Klan that operated in Muncie in the 1920s had been born as a twentieth-century hate group in 1915 in Stone Mountain, Georgia. Klan recruiters moved to midwestern and western states, including Indiana, hopeful of attracting new members. The Klan's first Indiana outpost was in Evansville in 1920, but the movement quickly spread to Indianapolis, the hub of KKK activity in Indiana, as well as cities like Muncie, Anderson, New Castle and Elwood.

At its height, the Klan claimed 240,000 members. Under the leadership of Evansville's D.C. Stephenson, the Indiana KKK helped elect two governors, two senators and many local officials in Hoosier cities.

The Klan's targets in the 1920s were Catholics, immigrants, blacks and Jews, Hoover wrote, and boasted that its goal was "100 Percent Americanism." The diversity of the objects of the Klan's hate meant that it could thrive even in cities like Muncie, where the minority population was only about 6 percent. Hoover wrote that Muncie's Catholic population of 7 percent pretty much equaled its minority population. Yet nearly one in twelve Muncie residents joined the Klan, Hoover noted.

Sometime in the spring of 1922, the Muncie chapter of the Ku Klux Klan organized, at the urging of local businessmen, during a meeting at the chamber of commerce. Hoover noted that the timing of the Klan's origin is confusing, since many believed it was organized to fight what some

Republicans considered a corrupt Democratic Party mayor, Rollin "Doc" Bunch. But by 1922, Bunch was already out of office. In 1919, two years into his second term as mayor, he was sentenced to two years in a federal penitentiary for mail fraud.

Bunch, granted parole after nine months and later pardoned, had come back to Muncie and ran for mayor in 1919 but was defeated by Republican John C. Quick. Dale, editor of the *Muncie Post-Democrat*, a weekly newspaper, began writing pointedly about the Klan in the spring of 1922. As Ron E. Smith, a journalism professor at the University of Central Florida, wrote in his 2010 essay for the *Indiana Magazine of History*, "The Klan's Retribution Against an Indiana Editor," Dale and his newspaper were "notable for engaging in an all-out editorial war with the hooded order and its 3,000 local members, exposing its secret membership rolls and ridiculing its silly rituals and anti-Catholic rhetoric."

According to Hoover, Muncie Klan members included Mayor Quick, Delaware Circuit Court judge Clarence W. Dearth, police chief Van Benbow, Delaware County sheriff Harry Hoffman, future mayor John C. Hampton and city council member Frank E. Barclay, who, Hoover said, was "Exalted Cyclops of Muncie Klan No. 4."

A Muncie City Hall fight broke out between Mayor Quick, who had left the Klan at some point, and KKK officials who wanted to fire some Muncie police officers deemed "not acceptable" by the Klan. Quick lost the battle and, Hoover wrote, the Klan controlled the police department—and Muncie City Council.

After recruiting Muncie members and staging nighttime parades to attract attention and invoke fear, the Klan found acceptance from individuals like the housekeeper for the prominent Jewish family of Martin Schwartz, who, as Hoover wrote, surprised and alarmed her employers by announcing that she had joined the Kamelias, the women's auxiliary for the Klan.

Other Jewish families felt the wrath—at least of an economic nature—of the KKK. Hoover wrote that the family of Sherman Ziegler, owners of a scrapyard, survived an attempt by the Klan to boycott Catholic- and Jewish-owned businesses.

Photographer Swift covered a June 1923 Klan march down Walnut Street of two thousand hooded and robbed Klansmen. Swift reported that ten times that many watched the procession. But the parade itself was a turning point in the public's perception of the KKK, Dale reported, with fights breaking out when many men in the crowd refused to take off their hats as a sign of respect.

Dale said that prominent Klan members began quitting the group, leaving the Muncie chapter at only about 1,500 members by the end of the year. The group split into at least two factions, with some prominent members, including a Methodist minister and former prosecutor, helping form the new group.

John C. Hampton, who had left the old Klan for the new Klan, was elected mayor after serving as jury commissioner for circuit court judge Clarence Dearth, a frequent target of newspaperman Dale's jibes. Dale wrote that Hampton had "packed" Dearth's juries with Klan members, Hoover wrote. The goal, Smith wrote, was to ensure that Klan members who were charged with crimes were not convicted.

Dale's *Post-Democrat* had alleged that Dearth and Hampton were protecting "certain dens of vice," Hoover wrote. Dale's newspaper had frequently targeted Dearth, and by 1927, Dale had been charged seven times, including at least one count of libel, in Dearth's court. Photos of Dale taken in the county jail show him smiling and defiant. At one point, Dale was convicted of contempt of court, fined $500 and sentenced to six months in jail. He didn't serve out much of the sentence but couldn't win exoneration in the case, which he pursued to the U.S. Supreme Court.

More than one account of the battles between Dale and the judge noted that Dearth told the newspaper editor that he should consider moving to Russia.

Ultimately, Dearth's seizure of copies of Dale's newspaper led to pleas from Muncie residents to the state that the judge be impeached. The effort failed, but Dearth's and Hampton's political careers waned after their battles with Dale received national attention.

During the height of the Klan's influence in Muncie, Dale aggressively criticized the group for, among other things, targeting a Catholic teacher in local schools. Dale had criticized so many local politicians, liquor sellers and gambling-den operators that what happened on March 22, 1922, could hardly be called a surprise.

In an incident that was covered in newspapers as far away as Baltimore, Dale said that he and his son were attacked by two men outside the newsman's home. A car with masked men inside pulled up to Dale's home and manhandled the older and younger Dales. During the struggle, Dale said, he tried to wrestle a gun away from one of his attackers. The gun went off, wounding the masked attacker. Dale said later that the subsequent funeral for a prominent Republican and Klan member indicated to him that the gunshot wound had been fatal.

In his *Indiana Magazine of History* article, Smith expressed skepticism, writing that some of Dale's encounters with the Klan had been embellished. "Although Dale's crusade against the KKK was undeniably courageous and justified, some accounts of the Klan's acts of retribution against him have been embellished so greatly that they oversimplify Dale's relationship with his community and mask his real accomplishments," Smith wrote. "Many of the embellishments can be traced to efforts to rally support for the embattled editor; others are the result of later observers misunderstanding the nature of the 1920s Indiana Klan."

Smith also noted, "Something of a showman, Dale contributed to this heroic image. As donations were being sought to defray his legal fees, he portrayed himself as a victim of Klan attacks and claimed to have killed a Klansman—who Dale said was a prominent Muncie citizen—during the 1922 attack. He even reenacted the encounter for Chicago newspaper photographers, and the pictures appeared in several newspapers. He took to wearing a hat with a bullet hole, presumably to demonstrate the poor aim of a trigger-happy Klansman. Hanging on his living room wall were the masks he said his attackers wore. He called them "Klucker scalps."

But Smith wrote that Dale had not yet really begun his newspaper attacks on the Klan at the time of the March 1922 attack. Dale wrote that the attack was "inspired by" his criticism of local corrupt politicians. (In Dale's obituary, the *Muncie Evening Press* reported with little elaboration that the former newsman and mayor had been "vilified, shot at and physically attacked.")

Smith noted that once Dale began newspaper coverage of the Klan, the articles were "unrelenting." The response was also strong: Dale was frequently confronted, even accosted, on the street. In 1926, bullets were fired into his house.

The Klan's influence was already lessening throughout Indiana by that time, caused in part by the 1925 arrest and conviction of Indiana KKK leader D.C. Stephenson for the rape and murder of Madge Oberholtzer. Hoover wrote that the "final blow" to the Klan in Muncie was Dale's election as mayor in November 1929.

If Dale's election was a surprise, it was particularly a surprise to the candidate himself, who in 1929 had said his fight with the Klan and other local forces had left him without a single friend. The election of Dale, who wasn't even a Muncie native (he had been born in Monticello, Indiana, in February 1869), was perhaps a reaction to his crusades and perhaps a reaction of voters tired of perceived corruption in Muncie government.

Dale had become involved in Democratic Party politics almost as soon as he came to Muncie in 1915, founding his newspaper and supporting Rollin H. Bunch's 1917 reelection campaign. Dale fielded an unsuccessful candidacy for the Democratic Party nomination for Indiana's governor and didn't find success until he ran for mayor of Muncie in 1929.

His 1936 obituary noted that his 1929 campaign was marked not only by articles in his own newspaper but also numerous radio speeches and public appearances, in which he attacked what he called corruption in local government. "Thousands flocked to hear the man who for years had been a crusader, who had lambasted corruption from the housetops, who had denounced the Ku Klux Klan," according to the obituary. "Into his campaign speeches he injected the same fire that had made his newspaper 'cussed and discussed' but read widely."

Dale, who had courted controversy throughout his time in Muncie, did it again on January 6, 1930, the day he took office. The new mayor forced the resignations of all forty-two of Muncie's police officers. The dismissal of ten firefighters seemed like an even bigger controversy, however, according to his obituary. And it was a costly controversy for Dale. Years later, courts ruled that eight of the fired firefighters were owed $80,000 in back pay.

Despite the election of several fellow Democrats to Muncie City Council, Dale never controlled the council and was more likely to feud with them. The mayor also clashed with the judge of Muncie City Court and ordered police officers to not file cases there.

Before Dale could mount an unsuccessful reelection campaign, more controversy struck. In March 1932, Dale and a dozen others were indicted by a federal grand jury on conspiracy to violate the National Prohibition Act, which outlawed liquor from 1920 to 1933. Dale was found guilty but maintained he was framed. In December 1933, he was pardoned by President Franklin Roosevelt.

In 1934, Dale lost his reelection bid to longtime associate Bunch, who had had his own controversies during his earlier time in the mayor's office.

His health failing, Dale spent the remaining fifteen months of his life quietly, his obituary noted. He was rarely seen on the downtown streets where he had become a notorious figure—hero to some and enemy to others. He died of a cerebral hemorrhage as he sat down to write an editorial for the latest edition of the *Post-Democrat*.

But Dale was certainly not forgotten, and neither were his battles. In 1979, the Ku Klux Klan conducted a parade through downtown Muncie. The marchers were fewer in number than they had been fifty-five years earlier,

Rollin Bunch (*left*) and George Dale shake hands. *Ball State University Digital Archives*.

and so were spectators, but *Muncie Star* editor Larry Shores wrote a column recounting Dale's exploits, including the night when he was attacked by but overcame supposed Klansmen.

After Dale's death in March 1936, his newspaper, the *Post-Democrat*, continued until March 1953. "Dale was a fighter and he made the Post-Democrat a fighter," the *Muncie Evening Press* wrote in 1953. Dale's son-in-law and a former Muncie mayor himself, Lester Holloway, announced the shuttering of the newspaper. When Holloway died in 1991, newspaper columns noted his four years as mayor, ending in 1951, and couldn't resist citing his father-in-law, Dale.

Before he moved to Muncie, Holloway had read about his future father-in-law's exploits in the *Chicago Tribune*. When he came to Muncie, Holloway had recounted in an earlier interview, he spoke to an ad salesman for Dale's *Post-Democrat*. "When he told me the editor was George R. Dale, I told him I would buy an ad and also asked if it would be possible to meet that man," Holloway recalled in the 1980s.

Holloway subsequently worked for Dale in both private business and at city hall and married Dale's daughter Betty.

Dale's death put him in national headlines again. The *New York Times*, a bastion of journalism that was about as different from the small, scrappy *Post-Democrat* as was possible, ran an obituary. "George Dale Dies: Ku Klux Klan Foe," read the headline at the top of page fifteen. "Elected after his battle with Invisible Empire had made him national figure."

## 6.

# "THE LUCKIEST GUY IN THE WORLD"

On the night of Friday, April 22, 1932, patrolman James Ovid McCracken laughed as he told his Muncie Police Department colleagues, "I'm the luckiest guy in the world."

At city hall that evening, McCracken and other officers drew lots to set the order in which the policemen could schedule their weeks off for the remainder of the year. McCracken was the winner and told his friends he planned to take the first two weeks of September off. Given that two nights later he would utter his last word—"North"—as he lay dying of gunshot wounds in a downtown Muncie street, McCracken's good-natured boast about his luck would take on a tragic irony.

But until his brutal slaying, few people would have disputed that good fortune had indeed smiled upon the thirty-five-year-old McCracken, known as both "Mac" and "Obie."

Since joining the police department more than two years earlier, he had become one of the city's most-respected and well-liked officers. But McCracken was also perhaps Muncie's most popular athlete of his day. The Tipton County native became a pitching phenom as a teen after his family moved to the Randolph County community of Lynn. McCracken's mound skills had nearly landed him in the major leagues a few years earlier.

Since 1930, he had been the ace on the pitching staff of the Muncie Citizens, the popular semipro team whose games often drew thousands of spectators to McCulloch Park.

Front-page newspaper coverage of the death of "Obie" McCracken. *Muncie Newspapers.*

His police job might have been an inducement for McCracken to move to Muncie and pitch for the Citizens, but colleagues and supervisors said he wore his badge—Number 59—and performed his law-enforcement duties with honor.

One would note that McCracken seemed more interested in resolving disputes among Muncie residents than in simply adding to his total number of arrests.

At the ballpark, and on his beat as a patrolman, McCracken made a lot of friends.

Bob Barnet, in the early years of a long career as sports editor of the *Muncie Star*, would write that McCracken was "known and loved by the newsboy on the street corner, the business head in the busy office." Barnet added, "He was a friend of the bootblack at the corner barber shop. He was a friend of the philanthropist."

It was not one of McCracken's routine tasks to accompany employees of the downtown Rivoli and Wysor Grand theaters when they delivered nightly deposits to the Delaware County National Bank in the 100 block of East Main Street. On the night of Sunday, April 24, however, the patrolman who usually drew that assignment was unavailable, so it was McCracken who followed Foster Norton, Wysor Grand manager, and Howard Webster, assistant manager of the Rivoli, as they carried their bags of cash bound for the bank.

The Great Depression had cost more than twelve million Americans—nearly a quarter of the nation's labor force—their jobs by 1932. Waiting for the Muncie theaters' money bags were four Indianapolis men who had turned to crime after losing their railroad jobs. Three of them hid in the darkness of doorways in the 100 block of South Mulberry Street. The fourth was behind the wheel of a getaway car parked nearby.

About 10:15 p.m., two of the bandits—later identified as Frederick E. Wildemann, thirty-five, and Russell Kramer Ijames, twenty-five—stepped out of the darkness and accosted the theater managers, pointing .32-caliber handguns at them and demanding their bags of cash.

When they realized their victims were being followed by a police officer, the gunmen grabbed Norton and Webster for use as human shields, then opened fire at McCracken. Witnesses said they heard as many as six gunshots. Two bullets struck McCracken in the chest.

"Mac never had a chance," Norton would say later that night. "He started backwards a few steps to try to get behind a car…and he couldn't make it. He staggered out into the street and fell."

There would be conflicting accounts over the years as to whether the police officer had managed to return fire. His service revolver remained in its holster, but a .25-caliber handgun he also carried was found underneath him in the street.

The top portion of Wildemann's left index finger was blown off by a bullet, but he would later acknowledge that the wound might have come from Ijames's gun rather than one fired by McCracken.

**Call Grand Jury to Indict Slayers of McCracken**

Edward H. Luker.        Donald Rohr.

Newspaper clipping of Edward Luker and Donald Rohr, slayers of "Obie" McCracken. *Muncie Newspapers.*

Another of the bandits, Edward H. Luker, thirty-eight, had apparently been assigned to physically confront any security guard accompanying the theater employees. However, he failed to do so.

The robbers dashed to their waiting car, clutching two bags that contained a total of $747 (more than $13,300 in 2018 currency). Their driver, Donald F. Rohr, twenty-five, sped north on Mulberry Street, in the process running over the fallen McCracken's right arm (his pitching arm). (Ironically, authorities would determine that Rohr, also a semipro baseball player, had played for an Indianapolis team against the Muncie Citizens, with Obie McCracken on the mound, the previous May.)

One of the theater managers tried to comfort the gravely wounded McCracken, while the other raced down Mulberry Street to city hall to get help. When two officers reached their fallen colleague's side, Obie McCracken said, "North," pointing up Mulberry Street, apparently indicating his attackers' escape route. He would say no more. The officer died a few minutes later in an ambulance en route to Ball Memorial Hospital.

An autopsy would show that the bullets had pierced McCracken's aorta, lungs and spleen. (He became the second Muncie police officer to die in the line of duty. The first, Toney Charles Hellis, was fatally shot while responding to a report of a domestic disturbance in September 1923. His assailant later turned his gun on himself.)

A large crowd gathered outside city hall, staying into the early morning hours, as news of McCracken's slaying spread through Muncie.

About 11:00 p.m., two city police cars were seen racing to investigate a report that a green sedan—similar to the description of the bandits' car provided by witnesses—had pulled along a gravel pit near the southern Delaware County community of Oakville. The *Muncie Star* reported that that effort turned up only a carload of romantic "petters," however.

The morning after the slaying, Sheriff Fred Puckett told reporters that his deputies would have been more than willing to assist in the search for suspects—but no one had told them about the homicide. "We could have had every road leading away from Muncie guarded within a few minutes," the sheriff said, adding that he hoped city police were successful in tracking down the killers.

"Wanted men do not always walk into the police station and surrender, however," Puckett added.

More distant law-enforcement officials apparently learned about the killing much sooner than did Delaware County's sheriff. During the predawn hours of April 25, police in Chicago questioned three men who had reportedly set fire to their own car about the Muncie slaying but found no connection. It would be the first of several reported breaks in the case that came to nothing.

Over the next several days, potential suspects were detained in Anderson—where a suspicious car had also evaded police after its occupants fired shots at a pursuing police officer—Elwood, Marion and, once more, Chicago, but all of those arrestees were eventually released.

The tombstone, in Woodlawn Cemetery, of James "Obie" McCracken. *Douglas Walker.*

Mayor George Dale referred to the fallen officer as "loyal and square." Police chief Frank Massey expressed frustration that the killers "wouldn't even give him a chance to draw and shoot it out."

"Mac was a wonderful man," Charley Gelbert, shortstop for the defending World Series champion St. Louis Cardinals—and a McCracken teammate in 1928 with the Rochester (New York) Red Wings—wrote in a telegram to his friend's window, Mabel.

(In the immediate wake of the shooting, and for years afterward, newspaper reports indicated McCracken had pitched in the major leagues. Eighty-five years later, Major League Baseball records reflect that he did not, at least in a regular-season game.

However, he was at times property of the St. Louis Cardinals and the Detroit Tigers, pitching for their farm teams as well as in independent leagues. His closest brush with the majors came in 1923, when he went to spring training with the Tigers, only to be cut shortly before the regular-season opener by Detroit's fiery player-manager, Ty Cobb. In eight minor league seasons—from 1922 through 1929, the year before he joined the Citizens—McCracken won eighty-six games.)

Obie McCracken's funeral—held at High Street Methodist Church, not far from the West Charles Street apartment the officer had shared with Mabel—drew a tremendous crowd, estimated at one thousand mourners. It was composed not only of Muncie residents but also scores of police officers—and baseball players—from across Indiana.

During the funeral, officers from Anderson, New Castle, Marion and Fort Wayne patrolled Muncie streets to allow McCracken's colleagues to bid the fallen officer farewell. Later, the procession of vehicles to Woodlawn Cemetery, east of Farmland in Randolph County, was reported to be two miles long.

Six days after the killing, management at the Rivoli announced that all proceeds from an 11:15 p.m. showing of *Cock of the Air*—an "aviation comedy" produced by Howard Hughes—would be given to Mabel McCracken. She had been named executor of her husband's estate, estimated at $700.

In the weeks and months after the slaying, Muncie police released few details of their investigation, but they traveled thousands of miles—across nineteen states and reportedly reaching the Mexican border—in pursuit of clues in the killing. One detective made a six-hundred-mile airplane flight to an undisclosed location.

The events that would lead to the capture of the Muncie officer's killers began to unfold on June 30, when a patrolman in Springfield, Ohio—thirty-six-year-old Charles A. Holt—was fatally shot in that city, about thirty miles northeast of Dayton.

On July 23, Ijames was arrested in Effingham, Illinois, in connection with the Ohio officer's death. He provided police with a statement in which he also admitted involvement in the Muncie robbery that led to McCracken's killing.

Based on information provided by Ijames, Luker and Rohr were arrested in Indianapolis on August 10, the latter at a local park as he prepared to play baseball. They were returned to Muncie and also provided confessions of sorts. That duo and Ijames—who remained in an Ohio jail—identified the fourth bandit as Wildemann, a former prizefighter who hailed from Mineral County, West Virginia.

His co-defendants also suggested that Wildemann had likely fired the shots that killed McCracken. In a jailhouse interview, Luker told the *Evening Press* that his family's desperate financial situation prompted him to accept an invitation from Ijames to participate in the Muncie holdup. "I've been out of work for two years," he said. "I'm man enough not to let my wife and kids go hungry....I was in a bad fix. I was about to be thrown out of my house because I couldn't pay the rent."

He maintained that he and Rohr "didn't expect anybody to be killed.... We're not guilty of murder. The law may say we are, but in the end, some time, up above, we will be judged innocent of taking a life."

Within three days of the arrests of Luker and Rohr, police chief Massey was circulating posters with Wildemann's photo and offering a $1,000 reward—provided by Muncie City Council—for information leading to his arrest.

Authorities believed that Wildemann was hiding in the West Virginia hills near his hometown of Keyser. "He's got to be in those knobs somewhere because his wife keeps taking food to him," said Massey, who traveled to the Mountain State to participate in the manhunt. But Wildemann—and another man linked to the Springfield slaying—were in New Orleans when they were apprehended on August 30. (The Indianapolis and New Orleans police departments would divide $770 of the $1,000 reward offered in the case. A Winchester attorney and Delaware County prosecutor Paul Leffler received the rest.)

In early September, Luker and Rohr pled guilty to second-degree murder and received life sentences from Delaware Circuit Court judge Leonidas

Guthrie. A few days later, McCracken's widow indicated that she wasn't entirely happy with the handling of their cases. "Naturally, I am full of hatred," she told the *Evening Press*. "If these men did not fire the shots that killed my husband, perhaps their punishment is just. But the men who actually killed should pay with [their lives] for my husband's life."

On September 26, the Citizens played a "McCracken Day" exhibition game that was reported to have drawn more than twenty thousand spectators to McCulloch Park. All proceeds from tickets and from souvenir badges bearing the pitcher's image—"expected to reach $400," an article said—went to their late teammate's widow. Providing the opposition that day were the "Reformatory Nine," a squad of prisoners from the Pendleton institution. The Citizens—who that season wore black armbands noting McCracken's absence—won the game, 10–1.

(Had he not three years earlier been granted a transfer to the Indiana State Prison, the Pendleton third baseman that day likely would have been John Dillinger, who had been one of the "Reformatory Nine's" best players for several years. As things turned out, Dillinger would visit Muncie, for non-baseball reasons, after his release from prison in 1933.)

On October 14, Russell Ijames pled guilty to murder in the Ohio patrolman's slaying. He was sentenced to life in prison and would never return to Delaware County to stand trial in McCracken's killing.

Ijames had given conflicting accounts of his role in the Muncie crime, saying at various times that he had stayed in the car during the holdup, was unarmed that night and that he had tried to shoot at McCracken but that his firearm had jammed. Ijames and a co-defendant in the Springfield case testified that they were part of a gang that had targeted theaters for robberies in Indiana, Ohio and Illinois.

Wildemann's case was transferred to Randolph County due to pretrial publicity, and he was held at the Indiana Reformatory in Pendleton for safekeeping. On February 28, 1933, the day his trial was to begin, he pled guilty to first-degree murder and was sentenced to life in prison.

On the witness stand that day, Wildemann insisted that he had not fired gunshots at the Muncie officer, saying Ijames and perhaps Luker were responsible for that. "I didn't shoot," he testified, "I did not have a gun. I don't know how many shots were fired. It sounded like an army to me."

A few hours later, however, while being driven to the Indiana State Prison in Michigan City, Wildemann acknowledged that he and Ijames had emptied their handguns while shooting at McCracken.

Mabel was again unhappy, firmly believing that Wildemann should have been sentenced to death. "You may think it's all right to let him off with a life sentence but it's different when it's someone in your own family," she told a reporter. "He'll try to get out on parole in a few years and then what?"

Her words proved prophetic. Luker and Rohr were granted parole by the Indiana State Clemency Commission in July 1942 after slightly less than a decade of incarceration.

Luker, then of Zionsville, died in 1962. Rohr, who had returned to a railroad job in Indianapolis, died in 1983. Later newspaper articles suggested that Wildemann was granted parole and released from prison in 1959. However, he had already been released by March 13, 1957, when he died at his home in Keyser, West Virginia.

Ijames—serving a life term for the Springfield officer's death—was released from an Ohio prison in May 1960 after that state's governor, Michael DiSalle, commuted his sentence. Ijames was living in Dallas, Texas, when he died in 1985.

As for Mabel McCracken, she told a reporter a few months after her husband's slaying that she wasn't certain she would ever be happy again. "For me, life seems to have stopped," she said. "I think I could only be happy again if I could join Mac 'over there'—if there is an 'over there.'

"I'd like to, but I guess one must…go on."

Mabel never remarried. She lived as a widow for nearly a quarter century before she died in December 1966. She was laid to rest next to Mac.

A niece who went through Mabel's keepsakes after her death found her late husband's baseball mitt, his Citizens uniform and yellowed newspaper clippings about his murder.

# 7

# THE DISAPPEARANCE OF FREDA LADURON

**J**ust what happened to Freda LaDuron is probably the most enduring Muncie mystery of all time.

Since 1937, it has lived on in the imaginations of people who never knew Jules LaDuron, prominent Muncie physician and political figure; in the memories of those who did; and, particularly, in the hearts of his family members. For them, it was more than a mystery. It was the special kind of sorrow when a beloved family member is widely rumored to have killed another.

For decades, it has lived on in schoolyard taunts, the reaction family members see when the LaDuron name is mentioned and with a granddaughter who tried to solve the mystery herself.

The years before September 16, 1937, were by most accounts low-key for Muncie physician Jules LaDuron and his wife, Freda Swanson LaDuron, a nurse who had graduated from school in Illinois and met her future husband at a Chicago-area hospital.

According to a complaint for divorce filed by Jules LaDuron many years later, Jules and Freda had married on April 12, 1928, about ten months after the doctor had been left a widower by his first wife's suicide.

As the wife of a physician, Freda LaDuron attended functions and appeared in the society columns of local newspapers, including "Society News," Ruth Mauzy's column in the *Muncie Evening Press*. Three years before Freda LaDuron disappeared, Mauzy wrote, the physician's wife was among those winning prizes for playing euchre at a meeting of the Semper Paratus

*Left*: Photo of Dr. Jules LaDuron on horseback, making rounds. *LaDuron family*.

*Below*: Photo taken in 2017 of the first house at Liberty Street and Orchard Place, where the LaDuron family lived when Freda LaDuron disappeared. *Keith Roysdon*.

Club. She was a member of several women's clubs. In February 1936, she represented her native country of Sweden at a meeting of the Muncie Business and Professional Women's Club.

The marriage of Jules and Freda LaDuron was typical of Muncie's elite—until it was not. The headlines in the *Muncie Evening Press* on September 25, 1937, said it all: "Wife of Muncie Health Officer Missing 10 Days"; "Relatives Unable to Locate Freda LaDuron."

Thirty-four-year-old Freda LaDuron had last been heard from on Thursday, September 16, when she told a relative she was planning to keep a dentist appointment. By September 25, Jules LaDuron was in an Indianapolis hospital, where he was being treated for an infected eye. Freda had left him three times before, always going to a relative's home before she returned, the physician said.

The September 25 article in the *Evening Press* noted that "a week ago," LaDuron had told an *Evening Press* reporter that his wife had left him after an argument, walking out of their home at Liberty Street and Orchard Place. What made Freda's disappearance newsworthy this time, however, was that she had left her two children, Suzanna, age seven, and Jacq, eight, behind with her husband; that she did not go to the home of a relative; and that her relatives, specifically two sisters from Illinois, raised concerns about her disappearance.

Selma Swanson, a sister from Galesburg, Illinois, came to Muncie to ask authorities to look for her sister. The Swanson family hired private investigators within days of Freda's disappearance. "Close friends of the woman are greatly concerned over her safety," the newspaper reported.

In the days that followed, Freda LaDuron sightings were reported in newspapers around the state and Midwest, although none of the sightings could be confirmed. Rumors circulated that she had returned to her native Sweden. There were also rumors that she had died at the hands of her husband.

Newspaper accounts counted up from the date she was last seen. "Health Officer's Wife Missing 13 Days," was the headline from one. The *Indianapolis Star* reported that immigration authorities had been called upon to help determine if she had left the country. The Indianapolis newspaper reported two theories: Freda LaDuron had moved somewhere and gone back into nursing; or she suffered from amnesia and was wandering... somewhere.

"She'll show up," Jules LaDuron was quoted as saying. "She always does." The physician told authorities that during the course of their marriage, his wife had left home for a week on one occasion and for two months on another.

As September drew to a close, Freda LaDuron was reported to have been seen in Seymour, Indiana, where she asked about the cost of an interurban train to Indianapolis.

Disquieting bits of information began to surface in October. After Jules LaDuron, in an Indianapolis hospital with an eye infection, urged police to search his home for clues to her disappearance, the *Muncie Star* reported, police found "considerable of her clothing was missing, including her nurse uniforms."

Attorney Clarence E. Benadum, a former prosecutor, was hired to represent Freda LaDuron's family members as the inquiry continued. "The attorney said he had served as counselor for Mrs. LaDuron

Portrait of Dr. Jules LaDuron. *LaDuron family.*

during domestic troubles, which she was having in recent years," the *Muncie Star* reported. "And he thought her relatives came to him yesterday with knowledge of that fact."

By early October, Freda's sisters, Selma Swanson and Hilda Johnson, and her brother, Ivar Swanson, were in Muncie to communicate a sense of urgency about the search. They also met with Jules LaDuron's parents, who were taking care of the children. Freda's siblings went to the prosecutor's office, accompanied by Freda's pastor, to urge action. They were told there was nothing that could be done except make their search for their missing sister orderly and systematic and consider offering a reward.

Out of nowhere, and most likely in response to rumors circulating throughout Muncie, newspapers reported that Jules LaDuron's eye infection was the result of penetration by a foreign substance while treating a patient on September 11. "Hospital attendants and his relatives emphatically deny that he is suffering of acid burns," newspapers reported.

On October 1, the *Muncie Evening Press* published this grim report: "Muncie police visited the LaDuron home again Friday afternoon and inspected a cistern (a water tank) under a room in the rear of the house. Lt. Detective August Felix is considering a proposal to have the cistern pumped dry. Sheriff Fred Puckett and police are attempting to investigate every report, regardless of how trivial it may seem."

On October 2, the *Indianapolis News* reported that the case of the missing woman "may be nearing a solution." The newspaper didn't say what prompted that report, however. A day later, the *Indianapolis Star* reported that Felix talked to a woman who said she saw Freda shopping in a downtown store on September 18, or two days after she disappeared. The woman hadn't come forward earlier because she thought she was doing Freda a favor by keeping quiet. Felix maintained that he believed Freda was at the home of friends.

On October 4, newspapers reported that Hilda Johnson had tried to visit her brother-in-law Jules LaDuron in his Indianapolis hospital room but was turned away.

The Swansons also issued a description of their missing sister—five feet, four inches, 132 pounds, light brown hair, slight Swedish accent—and urged the public to keep an eye out for her. They then returned to their homes in Illinois.

By early October, four people had come forward to say they had spotted Freda LaDuron in Muncie in the previous week. On October 16, a month after Freda LaDuron's disappearance, newsman Wilbur Sutton wrote a front-page column in the *Evening Press*. "This community cannot, or should not, have it said of it that a fine woman can just disappear as if a hole had opened up and she had been buried in it, unless we wish to have the reputation of not caring what happens to our people," Sutton wrote.

Newspaper advertisements were taken out aimed at Freda LaDuron, the *Indianapolis News* reported. The ads urged her to get in touch with her church's pastor. Friends and relatives would respect her wishes if she didn't want her whereabouts known, the ads noted.

In December, nearly three months after Freda's disappearance, Muncie police mailed five hundred postcards to police departments around the country. The cards included a photo and a description and noted a $200 reward offered by a fraternal organization.

By early 1938, Freda LaDuron's disappearance was becoming a Muncie cultural touchstone. In a February 1938 column, a visiting businessman is quoted as talking about the case over dinner, then asking, "Boys, will somebody please walk with me back to the hotel?" In April, newspapers reported that the discovery of the lower half of a woman's body on Lake Ontario, on the U.S.-Canada border, was ruled out as being connected to the disappearance. The dead woman was estimated to have weighed thirty to fifty pounds more than Freda.

In Cleveland, Ohio, thirteen people had fallen victim to a "mad slayer," and when a torso was found in that city in August 1938, police tried to determine connections, if any, to Freda LaDuron. But none were found. (The killer became popularly known in the media as the "Cleveland Torso Murderer.")

On September 16, 1938, the *Muncie Evening Press* published a story headlined, "Where Is She? No Answer to That Question" on the first anniversary of Freda LaDuron's disappearance. "Her friends are insistent that the search go on and they have spent liberally of their time and funds supporting it," the newspaper reported. "But today, one year later, there is no solution.

"Only the fact remains that a very widely known and highly esteemed young Muncie mother disappeared. Most of her relatives and friends now believe she is dead—but where, how and why?

"Many theories have been advanced, but all have failed to answer the question, WHERE IS FREDA SWANSON LADURON?"

In April 1939, Delaware County prosecutor Fred Davis made a surprising announcement: A grand jury would investigate the Freda LaDuron disappearance. A May 1939 *Indianapolis News* story reported that the investigation had been reopened and made cryptic reference to the search of the cistern beneath the LaDuron home.

At the time of the grand jury, which was to hear forty witnesses, the public heard a statement that Jules LaDuron made to a reporter weeks after his wife's disappearance. The physician said his grocery bill had gone down because his wife was no longer giving away groceries and that his children were happier than they were before their mother disappeared.

On June 4, the *Indianapolis Star* reported that the grand jury failed to reach a conclusion in the disappearance. In July, Ross Smith, described in the newspaper as "a Cincinnati deep diver," searched Mock's gravel pit, on the city's east side, for Freda with no luck.

SIGHTINGS OF FREDA LADURON still occurred but were infrequent as the years went on. Years after the fact, newspapers reported that when he was mayor, Rollin Bunch and his police chief said they saw Freda, working as a nurse, in a Chicago hospital only a few months after she disappeared.

But before many years had passed, newspaper coverage of Freda's disappearance was limited to articles noting the anniversary of her disappearance. A 1950 article on the anniversary again raised the issue of the cistern under the LaDuron house.

Jules LaDuron filed for divorce from the long-missing Freda in September 1945. In the filing, he swore that he had not seen Freda since September 16, 1937. By this time, their son, Jacq, was sixteen and daughter, Suzanne, was fifteen.

In ending his marriage to Freda, Jules took out a legal notice in the *Muncie Morning Star*, declaring his intention to divorce her and advising her to appear in court on November 14, 1945, if she wanted to contest the divorce. The ad appeared in print on September 15, 22 and 29, 1945.

In his effort to divorce Freda, Jules produced certificates from the army, navy and marines that Freda had not served in the U.S. armed forces in recent years. The effort convinced the court. In March 1946, Judge Paul Lennington granted Jules LaDuron his divorce from his long-missing wife.

Family members, eager to exonerate Jules LaDuron from any wrongdoing in his wife's disappearance, also tried to find Freda's whereabouts, even a half century or more later. In a 2017 interview, Leigh LaDuron, his granddaughter, said she made phone calls and went online to try to find her missing grandmother. Leigh came across the name Freda Greenspan in her searches. Leigh said the woman's age and background matched her missing grandmother's.

When Freda Greenspan died in Florida, where she had retired, her remains were returned to the Chicago area, where some of Freda LaDuron's siblings lived. Leigh spoke to Freda LaDuron's sister, whom she described as polite but not inclined to talk.

Her grandfather went to his grave maintaining that Freda had left and never came back. "Our grandpa didn't want to talk about it, but he knew she was alive and had disappeared," Jules, his namesake grandson, said.

## 8.

# THE MEAT MARKET MURDER

After the body of Lloyd C. Gleason was found on the floor of his Yorktown meat market's basement—on Monday, February 26, 1934—authorities quickly came to believe he might be the victim of a homicide.

It seemed like a logical assumption. The forty-year-old butcher had been shot twice in the head, and an attempt had apparently been made to stuff his remains into a furnace.

The body was discovered about 2:15 p.m. by Gleason's sister, Pearl Jefferson, who searched the premises after "she became alarmed at her brother's absence from the meat market" at Walnut and Smith Streets, the *Muncie Star* reported the following day.

The murder weapon—"a long-barrel .22-caliber pistol"—was found near the body. Coroner Clarence Piepho said the victim had been shot in the forehead just above his left eye and behind his left ear.

Gleason's left shoe and lower leg had been severely burned. Sheriff Otis Snodgrass said bloodstains found on the door of the furnace suggested that the burns were inflicted during a failed bid to place the body in the furnace.

Authorities acknowledged they suspected the butcher's son, twenty-one-year-old James Marvin Gleason, might know something about his father's final moments. The younger Gleason said he had brought his father's lunch to the meat market about 1:00 p.m. He also acknowledged to Yorktown marshal Otto Barker that he owned the gun found near his father's body.

"Gleason Killed by His Son"; front-page coverage of the Yorktown slaying. *Muncie Newspapers.*

Gleason—described by the *Muncie Evening Press* as "a thin, nervous and apparently bewildered youth"—was taken into custody the next day, when he "denied stoutly" he was responsible for his father's killing. The autopsy also revealed that Lloyd Gleason had cuts and bruises consistent with a beating.

Marvin recalled that when his mother, Dora, gave him the lunch he delivered to the butcher shortly before the slaying, she remarked, "I hope to Christ it kills him." He also maintained that he, not his Aunt Pearl, had later found his father's remains, which he described as "awful-looking, kind of hellish."

The younger Gleason could not account for a burn on his right palm.

Marvin described his dad as an abusive alcoholic, gambler and adulterer and said his own health had suffered as a result of his father's "drinking… [and] affairs with women." The son described a recent embarrassing incident that saw an intoxicated Lloyd Gleason chase "a Kentuckian living west of Yorktown all the way home and into his house."

Marvin described a time he and his mother were walking "past the Ford garage in Yorktown" when his father, intoxicated, backed out of the garage "hellbent for heaven" with two female passengers. "He hasn't run around with women as much lately as he used to," the son said. "He's not as frisky as he used to be."

Marvin denied ever contemplating killing his father. "When I left him at the store he was alive," he said. "And when I came back, he was dead. I don't know anything about it."

A few hours later, however, the younger Gleason admitted to the slaying. The confession apparently came after investigators found the bloodstained clothing Marvin Gleason had been wearing at the time of the slaying. Marvin said the shooting took place after his father ate his lunch, briefly left the meat market and then returned with a bottle of whiskey.

The pair fought as Marvin tried to take the bottle. He then went to the basement, retrieved his handgun and again confronted his father. A second struggle ensued and ended with the firing of the fatal gunshots. Gleason said he then dragged the victim's body to the basement and tried but failed to lift it into the furnace. He also shut off the flow of water to a nearby refrigeration unit, hoping that would somehow lead to an explosion that could conceal the cause of his father's death. "God bless his soul," a tearful Dora Gleason said after being told her son had confessed.

Marvin had been an honor student, graduating with the twenty-one-member Yorktown High School class of 1931 and performing in the senior class play, *Alabama Bound*. But he was primarily known as a loner. "Talk to him…and you could tell something was wrong," said an aunt. "We had known for a long time that his mind was bad."

Dora Gleason said she had tried to be "a pal" to her friendless son. She also took him to a psychiatric clinic in Detroit to be examined. A physician there "told us Marvin was in a very bad condition mentally" and recommended he be placed in a sanitarium in a western state, the mother said. The Gleasons could not afford to do that.

At one point after his high school graduation, Marvin moved into a room in the YMCA in downtown Muncie, but he had returned to his parents' home in Yorktown within a week. Dora said she hoped her son would be taken "to a place where they will be good to him and I think he will get all right."

On Wednesday, the younger Gleason remained in his cell at the Delaware County jail while his father's funeral was being conducted at Yorktown Methodist Church.

Marvin later would give a second statement concerning his father's death—in the presence of both his paternal grandfather and Sheriff Snodgrass. Those comments would result, on March 5—one week after the killing of her husband—in the arrest of Gleason's forty-year-old mother as an accessory in the slaying.

According to Marvin, Dora was aware that he had purchased the handgun and "had given him the idea of cremating the body a day or two before the murder was committed," the *Star* reported. "My mother has frequently made remarks to the effect that she wished my father were dead because he was drinking," Marvin said. "She has frequently said to me that she wished I would handle him or try to do something with him or else she would go crazy and do something herself.

"I had talked this all over with my mother…that I was to shoot him and cremate the body, that is, in so many words."

Asked by the sheriff about Marvin's allegations, Dora Gleason responded, "I'd hate to call him a liar."

Two days after her arrest, Dora pled not guilty and was released on a $10,000 bond.

Meanwhile, a pair of *Evening Press* sports columnists, Robert White and Dale Burgess, noted that Marvin had told police he was "too awkward to play basketball or any other game."

Recalling that a collection of paperback "luridly illustrated" dime novels had been found in the accused killer's bedroom, the sportswriters theorized that the younger Gleason's participation in athletics could have prevented the Yorktown tragedy. They suggested that if Marvin's remarks about being "too awkward" for sports "do not justify compulsory intramural athletics, nothing could."

In mid-March, a local grand jury launched an investigation into Lloyd Gleason's death. "This feels good, a lot better than being in jail," Marvin told a deputy who accompanied him from the jail to the courthouse for the grand jury proceedings.

A reporter noted that the bloody clothing worn by both the father and son on February 26 were in the sheriff's office, waiting to be displayed to grand jurors, along with Lloyd Gleason's charred left shoe.

On March 16, the grand jury indicted James Marvin Gleason on a first-degree murder charge. Gleason's mother was not indicted. (Two months later, prosecutor Paul Leffler would formally dismiss the preliminary charge that had been lodged against her.)

Marvin appeared at an initial hearing on the murder charge in Delaware Circuit Court on March 29. Asked by a deputy prosecutor whether he was guilty or not guilty, Gleason's only response was, "I don't know."

"The tall, slender youth was neatly dressed, but he retained the air of bewilderment noticeable since his arrest," the *Evening Press* reported.

Judge Leonidas Guthrie announced that he would appoint a "sanity commission" to determine if the Yorktown man was fit to stand trial. At a May 29 hearing, the commission—comprised of two Muncie physicians—persuaded Judge Guthrie that Gleason did not comprehend what he was accused of doing and could not assist in his defense should he stand trial. "He is not endowed by the mentality to carry on through life," Dr. L.R. Mason testified. "He's not interested in what they do with him. That is not normal. He probably would not pay attention to the proceedings if brought to trial."

An *Evening Press* reporter noted throughout the hearing that the "tall sandy-haired defendant sat slumped in his chair, with the fingers of his right hand concealing his eyes."

"Gleason is not normal mentally," Dr. Orville E. Spurgeon added. "I think he would know he was on trial for murder, but there would be a haziness in his mind.

"I think he knows he murdered his father. He sidestepped questions about the case at first, remarking, 'You probably know more about it than I do.'

"But he later said, 'I guess I killed him.'"

The physicians noted that Gleason graduated from high school with honors and received a scholarship to DePauw University but did not attend college. "He thinks other people do not recognize his ability and that he has not succeeded at things he has undertaken as well as he should," Spurgeon said.

Judge Guthrie ruled Marvin was "mentally incapable of standing trial" and ordered him confined in "the state colony for the criminally insane" at the Indiana State Prison in Michigan City. James Marvin Gleason would remain a resident of that colony for most of the next six years.

He returned to Delaware County, briefly, in March 1937 to try to convince Guthrie he was now capable of standing trial—a trial that would almost certainly see his attorneys maintain that the Yorktown man had been insane at the time of the 1934 slaying.

Dora Gleason by then had moved to Garrett in northeastern Indiana's DeKalb County, where she would soon marry a local chiropractor, Murray Ingalls. She and Ingalls told the judge they visited Marvin about every ten weeks and believed that his condition had improved.

However, while J. Frank Dowling, physician at the Delaware County jail, testified that he believed Gleason was now "capable of understanding," physicians Spurgeon and Mason—and a physician from the Michigan City colony—each said they still felt he was "lacking comprehension necessary" to stand trial.

Guthrie ordered Marvin Gleason returned to the state prison. The following October, a federal judge declined to intervene on Marvin's behalf.

Gleason's attorney, T. Ernest Maholm of Indianapolis, continued to work on his client's behalf, in 1938 suggesting that given the quality of mental health care at the prison "colony," authorities could "just as well have placed [Gleason] in a night club."

Things began to move in Marvin's favor in 1939, when Maholm won a change of venue that saw the murder case transferred to Randolph County. In December of that year, Randolph Circuit Court judge John Macy ruled that Gleason was now sane and set the Yorktown man's murder trial for February 26, 1940—coincidentally, the sixth anniversary of Lloyd Gleason's slaying.

On January 11, defense attorney Maholm filed a motion indicating that his client would pursue a defense of not guilty by reason of insanity. On February 7, Judge Macy agreed to release Marvin on a $2,500 bond, and that month's trial was put on hold. Gleason, free for the first time in three weeks shy of six years, apparently went to stay with his mother and stepfather in Garrett.

Sixteen months later, on June 5, 1941, Judge Macy granted a motion to dismiss the murder charge pending against Gleason. Delaware County prosecutor Thomas A. Cannon told the Randolph County judge "he didn't think there was a jury that would convict the man, and it would be a needless expense to have the trial." Gleason faced no further legal ramifications for killing his father.

But at some point over the next few years, James Marvin Gleason ceased to exist. Gleason changed his name to James Marvin Brady, adopting his mother's maiden name.

When Murray Ingalls—who had moved to Muncie in the late 1940s with Dora and, apparently, her son—died in May 1953, one of the survivors listed in his obituary was stepson "James Brady of Muncie." Eight years later, Dora Brady Gleason Ingalls passed away. Her obituary identified her surviving son as "Marvin Brady [of] Dallas, Texas."

In her will, Dora left son "James Marvin Brady" two-thirds of her estate, amounting to $7,125,09. (Dora's sister Ida received the other third.) His mother specified that a trust be established, with Marvin receiving his inheritance in the form of $100 monthly payments.

According to the Yorktown Historical Alliance, Marvin was referred to—perhaps both as Gleason and Brady, and by then living in Royse City, Texas—in yet another relative's will in the late 1960s. After his paternal aunt Pearl Gleason Jefferson died in 1968, she left him one or more pieces of local property.

The last local mention of Marvin—this time as Gleason, not Brady—apparently came in July 1982, when a *Muncie Star* column listed him among sixteen surviving members of his Yorktown High School class, which was celebrating its fiftieth anniversary one year late.

# 9.

# JULES LADURON AND THE CARTER BROTHERS

**S**hortly after 9:00 p.m. on Monday, November 6, 1950, a woman—never identified—reported in a call to the Muncie Police Department, "There's a terrible fight at Dr. LaDuron's office!"

"They're breaking glass and it's awful," the caller told city police sergeant Loren "Mouse" Alston. "Send the police!"

Almost as soon as that caller hung up, the MPD phone rang again. This time, Dr. Jules LaDuron was on the line. "Send police down to my office," he told Sergeant Alston. "I've just shot a couple of men."

Officers arriving at LaDuron's office, at 515 South Liberty Street, found its reception area and the physician's examination room in complete disarray, with furniture and equipment overturned and blood in puddles on the floor and splattered on walls. A dead man, victim of both a gunshot wound in the chest and an apparent beating, was on the floor. A second shooting victim, still alive, was nearby.

Jules LaDuron and his twenty-one-year-old son, Jacq—both showing signs of having engaged in physical battle—said the doctor had shot the men in self-defense.

The deceased shooting victim—officially pronounced dead, at the request of an officer, by Dr. LaDuron—was identified as twenty-seven-year-old Siebert "Pete" Carter, a Terre Haute resident who in recent months had been spending time in Muncie. The other man—with four or five gunshot wounds in his torso and blunt-force injuries to his skull—was Siebert's brother, thirty-five-year-old Ralph Winfield Carter.

In the years after the 1950 Carter shootings, Jules LaDuron moved his medical office to a building across the street. *Keith Roysdon.*

The mortally wounded Ralph fought with ambulance attendants on the ride to Ball Memorial Hospital, where he died soon after arrival.

Reporters from the *Muncie Evening Press* and the *Muncie Star* were apparently allowed to enter the homicide scene almost immediately. "Two Men Are Slain by Dr. LaDuron in a Terrific Battle at His Office," read the *Star*'s banner headline the following morning. Also on the front page was a large photo of investigators gazing down at the remains of Siebert Carter.

Authorities said the Carters had been extorting money from Jules LaDuron. "It was blackmail of a professional nature," police chief Harry Nelson told reporters.

At the scene, Jules LaDuron said that after an earlier fracas with Siebert Carter, both brothers "came at me," striking him with a wrench and repeatedly knocking him to the floor. At that point, he said, he retrieved a .38-caliber Smith & Wesson from his desk. "I shot Siebert first," he said. "Ralph was still coming at me, and I must have shot him three or four times."

At some point before he and Jacq accompanied police to city hall that night, Jules LaDuron reportedly told John "Jack" Ferris—longtime

*Left*: Siebert Carter. *Right*: Ralph Carter. *Muncie Newspapers.*

managing editor of the *Muncie Star*—that the blackmail had involved the 1937 disappearance of LaDuron's second wife, Freda. "It's a case of blackmail," LaDuron said, in Ferris's account. "This dates back to the time my wife disappeared. They have been blackmailing me ever since, by telling me they would let me know where she was if I would pay them. I just got tired of it and decided to end it tonight."

Later, Ferris would say that LaDuron called him the next day to report he had misspoken, that his dealings with the blackmailers had started only a few months earlier. For his part, LaDuron maintained that he had no memory of making any remarks to Ferris that night that concerned his wife's disappearance. (By this point, Freda was actually his ex-wife. In 1946, he had obtained a divorce from the missing woman and later took a third bride, Rena.)

That night, the *Star* reported that "hundreds of curious men and women" surrounded the Liberty Street house—the target of rumors and scrutiny in the wake of Freda's disappearance more than thirteen years earlier.

The next morning, news accounts of the mayhem in the doctor's office appeared in publications across the nation. "Two Men Slain by Physician," read a large headline stretched across the front page of the *Chicago Tribune*. A banner headline also greeted *Indianapolis Star* readers: "Muncie Doctor Slays 2."

After being questioned at city hall, Jules and Jacq LaDuron were both detained that night, held in cells at the Delaware County jail.

Jacq—a Ball State student who was married with a small child and still lived in the large house where his father practiced medicine—was released from custody on Tuesday. On Thursday, for reasons never explained, city officers went to the west-side campus and re-arrested Jacq, within view of classmates. The father and son were kept apart in the Delaware County jail and would not communicate for nearly four weeks.

Jules LaDuron retained the services of two well-known local lawyers—Leonidas Guthrie, who had served a term as Muncie mayor four decades earlier and later was Delaware Circuit Court judge, and John J. O'Neill, a former Jay County prosecutor.

On Friday, November 10, the defense team presented Delaware County coroner Samuel Drake with a thirteen-page signed statement from their client. In it, Jules LaDuron said that over the past five or six months, he had repeatedly been coerced into making cash payments—totaling $2,880—to a man he now knew to be Ralph Carter.

The doctor said both in phone calls and visits to his medical office that the man—identifying himself as "Kenneth Miller" of Terre Haute—persuaded LaDuron he was "a cold-blooded murderer or a gangster." In their first encounter, LaDuron said, "Miller" had implied that the physician's life would be in danger if he failed to give him money. LaDuron said the blackmailer had also "mentioned that I had an unfortunate experience with a lot of notoriety some years before and it was to my advantage to avoid any more."

"Miller" returned three or four weeks later and demanded more cash, threatening to "bring out some scandal about my wife's family." The blackmailer left the office that day with $750. He would demand, and receive, cash payments on at least two other occasions over the next several weeks.

Jules LaDuron, then fifty-seven, did not have a reputation as a man who could be easily intimidated. At the time he was being blackmailed by Ralph Carter, the doctor explained, he was "in a bad mental condition because of my mother's imminent death." (Jemina Joris LaDuron had died at age seventy-three on September 28.)

On November 6, LaDuron said, it was another man—later determined to be Ralph's brother Siebert—who came to his office demanding cash. The physician said that man—identifying himself as "Alvin Carver" of New Castle—repeated a claim he had made to LaDuron in an earlier phone call. He said he wanted the doctor to pay for his wife's medical expenses stemming from an abortion LaDuron had purportedly performed on her the previous May.

Jules LaDuron had had enough. He called "Carver" a "damned liar" and said he intended to call the local prosecutor's office. Jules said Siebert Carter then attacked him, and they engaged in an extended brawl. After he subdued his assailant, the doctor said, Jacq came into the office. The physician determined that "Carver" was an associate of "Kenneth Miller," who was waiting outside in a car.

LaDuron said he washed blood from his nose and mouth, combed his hair and saw three patients who had been in the waiting room. He then asked Jacq—who at his father's request had been keeping an eye on the battered Siebert Carter—to go out and ask his accomplice to come inside. When Ralph Carter saw that his brother had been beaten, he "rushed at me like a mad bull," Jules said.

The physician said that both Carter brothers—armed with a wrench LaDuron had brought to his office for protection and stirrups removed from an exam table—began to pummel him, knocking him down again and again. (Jacq LaDuron would later testify that he had been knocked unconscious as the melee began.) It was then, Jules LaDuron said, that he retrieved his handgun from a desk drawer and began firing. Siebert was shot in the chest and went down. Ralph Carter took four bullets and remained standing, the physician said, prompting him to repeatedly hit the Terre Haute resident in the head with the barrel of his gun. "That is enough," Ralph Carter told LaDuron as the Terre Haute man finally collapsed. "I am done for."

Investigators would determine that Ralph Carter had targeted other physicians—in cities including Anderson, New Castle and Chicago—for blackmail, usually with claims that involved purported abortions. A member of his extended family admitted that she had written an extortion letter to a Chicago doctor at Ralph's request. Married and the father of four children, Ralph had compiled an arrest record for crimes ranging from assault and battery to malicious trespass. Siebert Carter's record, meanwhile, appeared to be limited to a "vehicle taking" case that dated back to his teens.

Authorities said the Carters had been staying with relatives in Muncie in recent months, for a time each working at the Chrysler plant in New Castle.

Jules LaDuron and his son would remain in the county jail for most of November as prosecutor Guy Ogle—in his last weeks in office, having been unseated in the previous May's Democratic primary—prepared to take the case to a grand jury. In the meantime, the probe into Freda's 1937 disappearance suddenly came back to life.

Freda's sister Selma Swanson of Galesburg, Illinois, publicly called for a reexamination of her sister's fate. "Recent newspaper articles renew my conviction that someone somewhere knows her whereabouts or the circumstances of her end," Selma wrote in a release. On November 10, Muncie police began to dig at what was called an "unmarked grave" in a Gaston-area cemetery, "reported to contain the remains of the long-missing woman," according to the *Evening Press*. However, that effort apparently failed to produce a body – that of Freda or anyone else.

By November 13, Chief Nelson—who had maintained that the 1937 mystery and the more recent slayings at the doctor's office were unrelated—said that he had "all available men working on the [Carter] case."

A dozen days later, however, Indiana State Police searched the Liberty Street property "in an apparently futile attempt to reopen the Freda LaDuron case of 13 years ago," the *Muncie Star* reported. As Muncie police and LaDuron's attorneys looked on, ISP investigators "went over the masonry construction of the LaDuron basement virtually brick by brick." The troopers were specifically looking for a tunnel that informants claimed had attached the basement to a fruit cellar. None was found.

After seventy-five minutes, the state investigators declared that they had found nothing to justify "extensive and difficult digging operations" in the house's basement. "If there ever was a tunnel, it has been filled in for a hell of a long time and the dirt is hard as concrete," Chief Nelson said. Jules LaDuron—who from jail had agreed to the search—said he had also heard reports of a tunnel but never found one.

The *Muncie Star* reported that "an Indianapolis newspaper" had put pressure on state police to reopen the Freda investigation. Testimony before the grand jury—about the Carter shootings, not Freda's fate—began on November 30. That day, Jules and Jacq saw each other, in the courthouse hallway, for the first time since the night of the killings. Grand jurors, driven in police cars, went to LaDuron's office. One found a bullet mark on a medicine cabinet that had apparently not been noticed by police.

On December 6, the grand jury indicted Jules LaDuron on two counts of manslaughter, each carrying a prison term of from two to twenty-one years. The physician that day posted a $10,000 property bond and was released from jail. Jacq, who was not charged with any crime, had been released from custody a few days earlier. (More than six decades later, a relative still recalled the young father emotionally holding his baby son when he arrived home that day.) The physician would not stand trial on the charge stemming from Ralph Carter's death until January 1952.

LaDuron's testimony on the witness stand would be consistent with the lengthy statement he had provided to the coroner fourteen months earlier. The physician said that during one of his early encounters with Ralph Carter, he was warned that a failure to pay might result in him being found "in a ditch with a bullet in your guts."

He recalled that as the Carters were beating him with the metal stirrups, Ralph told his brother, "Let's kill the S.O.B.!"

"Things happened so fast, so furiously," the doctor said of his struggle with the brothers. "Everything was so desperate."

During the fracas, he recalled, LaDuron wondered, "Where the devil is Jacq?" He then saw his son, knocked unconscious, sprawled on the office floor. "I thought he was dead," LaDuron testified, as he fought to retain his composure. "I thought they'd killed my boy."

Asked by prosecutor Bernell Mitchell—elected the day after the 1950 killings—why he had not told police about the blackmail scheme, LaDuron said that he had "no confidence in the police helping me when I was in trouble." He said that earlier reports he had made to police—about an investment scam involving silver foxes and break-ins at his property—had not resulted in legitimate investigations.

Witnesses said LaDuron's gun holster was found stuffed into the dying Ralph Carter's pants. A police officer, Walter Boguske, testified that the physician had tried to persuade him the gun he used to shoot the brothers had belonged to Carter. LaDuron said he didn't know how Carter ended up with the holster. He denied ever indicating the gun was not his.

While the doctor testified, a photographer from an Indianapolis newspaper used a noisy "speed-light flash gun." The defendant turned to judge Joe Davis. "I'm going to ask the man in charge here to stop this clicking of pictures while I'm on the stand," the physician said.

"You heard what he said," the judge told the photographer.

Witness Bula Allen said she saw a man "knocked through that [glass] door" on the north side of the LaDuron building, and that he was "definitely hollering for help" as he was dragged back inside. At some point during that evening's violence, Jacq LaDuron testified, Siebert Carter had crashed through a window, and his father instructed him to bring him back inside.

Judge Davis allowed little testimony from other physicians who said Ralph Carter had extorted money from them with claims of abortion. Jurors did hear that a "little black book" containing the names of several physicians was recovered from the ambulance that transported Ralph Carter to the hospital.

Nine witnesses took the stand to attest to Jules LaDuron's good character. Claude Jones, a local locksmith, testified that the Carter brothers had responded with "cussing and threats" when he asked them to stop throwing their beer cans into his mother's North Pershing Drive yard.

*Muncie Evening Press* trial coverage included sidebars that touched on the main players' attire and descriptions of "wintry light filtering in from the long windows at the old-fashioned courthouse [casting] a somber glow."

Testimony in the case began on a Tuesday. By Friday, both sides had presented their evidence. In his closing argument, Mitchell asked, "Is a killing ever justified because the man who was killed was a bad man? The lives of a mother's sons were extinguished and their souls catapulted into eternity. Their lips are sealed by death."

Defense attorney O'Neill called Ralph Carter "as cunning as a leopard, as slimy as a snake…running his business as a blackmailer the way you'd operate an automobile assembly line."

"If any man can blacken those fellows' reputations any blacker than they were in Terre Haute and here, I don't know how you'd do it.

"I venture to say Al Capone wouldn't have wiped his feet on a scheme like Ralph conceived. We'll never know how many doctors he started in on. We'll never know the heartache and pain he caused."

O'Neill urged jurors to "not say to the world that Delaware County's going to make a safe place for the blackmailers."

Deputy prosecutor Harry Redkey maintained that LaDuron should not have taken the law into his own hands. "Never once did he raise his voice or his hand to the law officers of Delaware County for his protection," Redkey said.

Guthrie, the former mayor and judge, told the jury to tell the world "it doesn't pay for people like Ralph Carter and his brother to come into Delaware County and pull any of their shenanigans."

On the morning and afternoon of Saturday, February 2, 1952, the Delaware Circuit Court jurors deliberated for three hours and nine minutes before reporting that they had a verdict.

About three hundred people were in the courtroom at 2:40 p.m. when Judge Davis announced that Jules LaDuron had been found not guilty. Many of those present cheered. "It was a spectacular ending of one of the most widely publicized murder trials ever held in the Delaware Circuit Court," the *Muncie Star* reported.

Rena LaDuron clutched her husband, embraced her sister-in-law and sobbed when the verdict was announced. "It doesn't look like it, but I feel wonderful," she told a *Star* reporter.

Jules accepted congratulations from most of the occupants of the packed courtroom. "I was confident," he said. "Of course I'm very happy the way it all turned out."

After a week in the courtroom, LaDuron said he looked forward to being able to resume normal office hours. He had met with his patients, as time permitted, during breaks in the trial. "I think it came out just right,' Jacq LaDuron told reporters. "That was justice." (The younger LaDuron went on to become a longtime Muncie pharmacist. He also, to Jules LaDuron's delight, would father four more children. Jacq died in 1979.)

Two days after the verdict, Mitchell told the *Star* it was unlikely Jules would stand trial on a manslaughter charge stemming from Siebert's death. "The state lost and I can see no reason for playing the same record over and putting the county to the expense of another trial," he said. The chance of new evidence surfacing "is remote in my opinion," the prosecutor added.

Mitchell would formally drop the remaining manslaughter charge on March 26, noting that it would have cost the county between $700 and $1,000 to conduct another trial. "The ends of justice," Mitchell said, "would not be served by trying Dr. LaDuron a second time."

## 10.

# ENTER AT YOUR OWN RISK

Over the decades, Muncie's taverns served up cold beer and hot death. From the city's earliest days until the end of many neighborhood taverns and hole-in-the-wall bars as the community's industrial age faded—taking workers and their paychecks with it—Muncie's bars and watering holes were known as a good place to have a cold brew, meet your future spouse and gamble…sometimes with your life. Tavern patrons, with a bellyful of beer or whiskey, were known to start a fight, only to be thrown out of the premises by the bartender or bouncer.

In July 1953, however, mayhem came from behind the bar, when bartender Delmo Cooper allegedly shot and killed Melvin Grubbs outside the Fireside Inn, on U.S. 35 South, just outside the Muncie city limits. Initial accounts indicated that Cooper, who confessed to the shooting early on but was acquitted in two separate trials in the years that followed, was incensed that Grubbs used vulgar language in front of Cooper's wife. But testimony that followed indicated a more complicated, personal beef on Cooper's part.

The shooting occurred on Cooper's twenty-eighth birthday. Grubbs was twenty-three. Newspaper accounts focused to a great extent on Cooper's looks, noting in the second paragraph that he was "ruggedly handsome." Also noted was that he was "dressed neatly in a white shirt and well-pressed trousers."

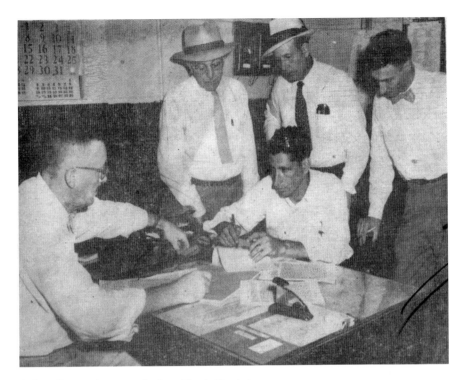

Delmo Cooper signs a confession. *Muncie Newspapers.*

THE SHOOTING AT THE Fireside Inn was not the first fatal encounter at the establishment. In September 1948, twenty-seven-year-old Carl Eugene "Jack" Gibson was shot to death after an argument and struggle with some Madison County men who had come to the inn looking for an after-hours spot to drink and play poker. Gibson and his wife, who worked at the Fireside Inn and lived nearby, heard a car outside after 2:00 a.m. and went out, only to be confronted by the men.

Police believed that, during a struggle, Gibson and Hobart Merritt of Frankton fought over a gun. Gibson held the gun by the barrel and struck Merritt with it, causing a skull fracture. The gun discharged, fatally wounding him in the chest. A grand jury issued no indictments in the incident.

"Two Dead in Shooting; Police Kill Slayer" screamed the headlines in the *Muncie Evening Press* on May 5, 1958, when thirty-six-year-old Lee Jeter went on a rampage on Muncie's near south side. Police said Jeter first shot and killed his live-in girlfriend, twenty-six-year-old Jane Alice Jones, then went to a Second Street café, where he fired several shots from a single-barrel shotgun into the building. Jeter, on foot, then encountered sixty-year-old

Prentice Gilmore, an unemployed hotel porter, outside Bob's Tavern. Jeter fatally shot the man.

Muncie police officers Claude "Jack" Hines and Marion Gibson Jr., on the police force for a little more than a month at the time, had been sent to the café on the shooting call. When they arrived, Jeter started shooting at them. They returned fire, killing Jeter. Newspaper photos depict the body of Gilmore, covered by a sheet, on the ground outside the tavern.

The police officers' actions were ruled justifiable, although authorities acknowledged that Jeter's shooting rampage might have been prevented if they had found the man hours earlier, when police first received reports that he was carrying a gun at the corner of Monroe and First Streets.

The city's cafés and the roadhouses outside of town could also be dangerous places. In March 1960, Jesse J. Gibson, owner of the Dark Moon Restaurant on U.S. 35 south of Muncie, was charged with the shooting death of twenty-three-year-old James Greer. Gibson said Greer had caused trouble at his establishment for more than a year and had been barred from the café. But Greer returned one night with two other men. Gibson gave Greer two minutes to leave before pulling a snub-nosed .38 revolver out from under the bar.

After Greer was shot and Gibson was arrested, the café owner told police, "It's the only thing I knew to do. You don't know the trouble I've had with him the last year or two."

The *Muncie Evening Press* said Gibson was "a small man with a determined expression."

One witness said he heard the shot and then Gibson shout, "Damn you, now do you believe I'll shoot you?"

As the investigation into the incident continued, Greer proved to have been well known to police, with numerous arrests for public intoxication and disorderly conduct. His record extended back to several juvenile incidents. Nearly two years before the shooting, Greer had been arrested in May 1958 for shooting out the neon sign on Gibson's café.

During Gibson's trial a few weeks later, in July, his defense attorneys cited a police photograph showing a "bowling machine puck" near Greer's body, possible evidence that the soon-to-be-killed man had planned to use it as a weapon. But police officers said they had placed the puck in the picture to help them focus the camera.

More than fifty defense witnesses were called to testify as to Gibson's character, and the jury—five women, seven men and two alternates—was taken to the Dark Moon to look at the scene.

In mid-July, after two weeks of testimony, Gibson's trial ended in a hung jury. After more than twelve hours of deliberations, jurors were deadlocked in a 10–2 vote in favor of acquittal.

Defense attorney Clarence Benadum, a veteran Muncie lawyer, delivered a ninety-minute final argument.

*It was the spectacle of Benadum in action that many in the overflow crowd had come to see. Benadum began by crushing the onus of the name Jesse James Gibson, by justifying it with Biblical scriptures…and continued to quote from Shakespeare three times, Jesus Christ once, other Biblical sources six times, a Klondike poet once and even once from a law book.*

*He thundered and he wept. He lay on the floor to demonstrate the position of Greer's body next to the steel puck that had been photographed at Greer's head. He bent over the prosecution table and wagged a "naughty boys" finger. He brought the Gibson family to tears time and again.*

As August began, Gibson was released from jail, for the first time since the shooting, on $20,000 bond. Prosecutor Gene Williams "took the decision [to free Gibson] as a near-crippling blow in the state's chances" for conviction in a second trial, if one was to be held.

Newspaper coverage of the slaying of Willie Price. *Muncie Newspapers.*

THIRTY-FOUR-YEAR-OLD WILLIE OSCAR PRICE walked into the Magic City Tavern, in the 600 block of South Walnut Street, on February 21, 1964. Within minutes, Price was dead, his throat slashed from ear to ear, and twenty-seven-year-old James Mullinix was under arrest.

Authorities were puzzled as to what had happened to cause Mullinix to attack Price. The tavern was crowded shortly after 1:00 a.m., and other patrons recounted seeing Mullinix and another man stand and walk up to Price. A moment later, Price was on the floor of the bar. Mullinix and his companion fled from the bar. Mullinix ended up in the Yorktown home of a friend, where police found him within minutes. Mullinix came out and asked, "Did the guy at the Magic City die?"

After a seven-day trial, Mullinix was found guilty of manslaughter. Throughout his trial, Mullinix admitted that he had had a "scuffle" with Price but denied cutting the man's throat. "The only way he was cut was with his own knife because I didn't have a knife," Mullinix testified. "I did not cut Willie O. Price."

A bartender testified that he saw Mullinix "put his arms around victim's neck" before Price fell to the floor.

In March 1965, Mullinix was sentenced to from two to twenty-one years in the state prison system.

A side note from Mullinix's trial had to do with how many liquor establishments were open and available the night of Price's slaying. An officer testified, "There were 35 taverns and seven package stores along the route driven by Price and two companions before they reached the Magic City the night of the crime, and 10 taverns within one block of where they parked their car."


IN 1970, A BAR not all that far from the Magic City was the scene of a fatal shooting in the midst of New Year's revelry. Harold D. Hughes, twenty-two, was shot in the chest in what newspapers called a "New Year's Eve fracas" just outside the Neptune Bar, in the 1400 block of South Walnut Street.

Police quickly arrested Alfoncer Charles Wayne Watson, a twenty-two-year-old member of the Titanics, a band that was playing at the Neptune that New Year's Eve. Police said a fight broke out inside the bar. Hughes had parked his car and "walked into the turmoil" but apparently was not a target. Hughes had been, however, barred from the Neptune Club months earlier for attacking a musician at the club.

Watson pled guilty to voluntary manslaughter rather than a charge of second-degree murder and received a two-to-twenty-one-year prison sentence.

The slayings in Muncie taverns put a particularly bloody punctuation mark to the checkered history of the establishments in Muncie.

In May 1946, despite the warnings of Indiana alcoholic beverage officials, illegal gambling, including paper "tip" books, was common in Muncie bars and taverns. Later that year, writer Charles Griffo reported on the rampant sale of tip books—paper gambling devices, in effect, that remain popular in some bars to the present day—and noted that they were "practically a Muncie institution" and a source of income for bar owners. "Muncie is usually credited with being the tip book center of the world," Griffo wrote.

In April 1947, the state alcoholic beverage commission lashed out at Muncie taverns, saying that too many establishments didn't serve food as required, had lighting that was too dim and let minors enter.

The Muncie Tavern Owners Association went on the defensive, posting signs threatening minors with arrest if they entered their establishments and arguing that Muncie's taverns were clean and well lit. Later that year, the tavern owners were still fighting criticism from state excise police. "We've almost got the juvenile problem whipped, but there are still a few underage persons who try to slip into taverns, especially on the outskirts of the city," Jerry Justice, president of the tavern owners group, told newspapers.

The bar owners came up with a plan: "a blacklist for juveniles, professional drunks, 'finks' and police characters will be circulated weekly among local taverns by the tavern owners themselves," the *Muncie Evening Press* reported.

By June 1947, authorities announced a plan to license waiters and waitresses in taverns—noting that those servers could be fined or lose those licenses if they were caught serving minors or otherwise breaking state law. Bartenders were already licensed in that manner. Waitresses could lose a "lucrative $40 to $50 a week job," officials noted.

The tavern battle was still being waged in 1949 when the *Muncie Evening Press* noted a crackdown on gambling and other tavern activities. About gambling, the paper wrote, "Tavern owners might as well forget about this business, this racket which for too many years ran unmolested in Muncie. The people have had enough of it and they want no more."

The city's taverns continued to be a rough-and-tumble world, however. Right before Christmas in 1950, a seventeen-year-old girl pulled a knife on Muncie patrolman Melvin Miller outside a South Walnut Street tavern. The girl, who said she had turned seventeen a month earlier, said that she was married and was the mother of a two-year-old.

Police believe she was intoxicated, but the girl wouldn't admit that she had been drinking in one of the taverns up and down the stretch of street.

## 11.
# THE COPS WHO WOULDN'T STOP

**A**s two of Muncie's first African American police officers and investigators, Melvin Miller and Ambrose Settles were often on the front lines in the fight against crime.

The two were among several officers called in on December 10, 1952, when the body of sixty-two-year-old Helen Griffith was found on the floor of her house in the 800 block of Macedonia Avenue. Griffith, quickly labeled a "spinster" in newspaper accounts, was found in a pool of blood in a room she rented to seventy-four-year-old Charles Smith, who found his landlady upon returning from a trip to the grocery store.

Griffith had been stabbed several times with a sharp knife, authorities said, although she was killed by a wound more than two inches long to her throat that severed veins and an artery. Griffith was not "criminally assaulted," a euphemism that the initial newspaper account used, but she had been "manhandled." Her jaw was bruised and several teeth were loosened. Her purse, with seventy-one dollars in it, was left untouched in her room. Her cat walked through the pool of blood around Griffith's body and left bloody paw prints around the house.

Police detectives were already working on a murder that had occurred just two weeks earlier: Lewis P. Laveck, a seventy-three-year-old shopkeeper, had been robbed and killed in his store on Memorial Drive. Three men had been arrested and were being held in that slaying.

Smith was quickly eliminated as a suspect in Griffith's killing when police confirmed his alibi: He had been playing cards in a downtown tavern at

**Detective Story Magazine Features Local Patrolmen**

Patrolmen Melvin Miller, right, and Ambrose Settles look over a current issue of a detective magazine which tells of their six-year search for the slayer of Helen Griffith of Muncie in 1952.

Muncie police officers Melvin Miller (*right*) and Ambrose Settles look at a detective magazine story about their pursuit of a killer. *Muncie Newspapers.*

the time of his landlady's killing, leaving the game to pick up groceries and return to his room in Griffith's house, only to literally stumble over her body.

A picture of Griffith began to emerge. Before she was killed, she had retired from a city parks department job, liked to play piano in a store that sold sheet music and made loans to people who were down on their luck. She had loaned as much as $150.00, and would charge about $0.75 in interest on a $3.00 loan—if she charged any interest at all. Sometimes, she did not.

Five suspects were questioned in connection with Griffith's death, and police at one point said another woman might be a suspect. Two men were released after they passed lie-detector tests administered by Indiana State Police. Police theorized that someone who had borrowed money from Griffith—or tried to borrow money but was refused—committed the murder. Griffith owned a few properties in the Whitely neighborhood but had an estate valued at only a little more than $2,000 that was divided between fourteen cousins and an uncle.

Weeks turned into months, and months turned into years before Griffith's slaying was solved by Miller and Settles.

In October 1958, nearly six years after Griffith's murder, news broke that twenty-eight-year-old James Anderson had been arrested. Newspaper accounts of his arrest featured a picture of Miller and Settles and the secondary headline, "2 Policemen Finally Get Confession." The arrest climaxed "an interesting story of an investigation which two Muncie police officers continued after the case was forgotten by many," the newspaper article read. "Anderson's arrest topped off years of hard work and personal expense by Patrolman Melvin Miller and Sgt. Ambrose Settles, despite skepticism on the part of some fellow officers."

The two cops were called out right after the murder to work the streets in the predominately black neighborhood where Griffith, who was white, lived.

Two years after Griffith was killed, Miller was told that Anderson was in the vicinity of Griffith's home the night of the slaying and was overheard talking about bloody gloves in a telephone call.

The cops continued their investigation. Two years later, in 1956, Miller and Settles took a trip to Los Angeles on vacation. But during that time, the investigators questioned a man who had left Muncie shortly after Griffith's slaying. A lie-detector test administered by L.A. cops cleared the man, however.

The man, who had a record of public indecency charges, returned to Muncie and was arrested. But a woman came to Miller's home to identify another man, Anderson, as the killer. Miller wrote to friends in Chicago, Detroit and Dayton, trying to find Anderson. The detective learned that Anderson was in prison in Michigan on a burglary charge. He was due to be released in November 1957. At first, Miller believed that Anderson was going to Chicago after his release from prison but later heard that he was headed for Dayton.

Miller took a Muncie police car to Dayton, where he was assisted by three black cops in searching for Anderson, who could not be found. Anderson ultimately returned to Muncie but laid low for a few days. Miller found Anderson and persuaded him to come to his home, where the two drank coffee for four hours. Anderson maintained that he had left Muncie because he had assaulted his grandmother, but Miller determined through police records that that incident had occurred nine months before Griffith was killed.

Miller arrested Anderson and, after several hours of questioning at the Delaware County jail, got Anderson to admit he had killed Griffith. In a written confession that he later recanted, Anderson said he had gotten off work at the Broderick Company plant on December 10, 1952, bought some wine and drank it all. He said he didn't have money to buy more but remembered hearing about a woman in Whitely who loaned money.

Griffith refused to loan Anderson three dollars because she didn't know him and told him to leave, but Anderson said he pushed his way into her house and a struggle ensued. "The lady finally made me mad, as I was trying to calm her down, not harm her," Anderson told police. "During the fighting, I lost my head and took my knife out of my pocket....I opened the knife and stabbed her in the throat."

A local grand jury indicted Anderson on a second-degree murder charge. He pled guilty to voluntary manslaughter and was sentenced to prison in November 1959.

In August 1960, a state parole board denied his bid for release from his sentence of from two to twenty-one years. In November, a *Muncie Star* article noted that Miller and Settles and their six-year pursuit of Helen Griffith's killer was fodder for an article in an unnamed detective magazine. The two cops were shown looking at copies of the magazine.

With such aggressive police work sometimes came complaints. In *Life on the Color Line*, Gregory Williams's autobiography about moving to Muncie and finding out his racial heritage was African American and not Italian, as his father had told him, Williams recalls an incident when Settles stopped him and his father on the street to question his father about a burglary. Williams's father was not involved in the burglary but did have information about it that came out after Settles roughed up the older Williams and sent Greg Williams running home.

In September 1963, Settles died at the age of forty-seven after what the obituary called an extended illness. The obituary for the Kentucky-born Settles cited the years-long effort by him and Miller to solve Helen Griffith's murder.

Miller continued to be active in the Muncie community near the end of the twentieth century, working within the Democratic Party but offering up skepticism about the local political process. At one point, he took a reporter to a local nursing home to introduce him to residents of the home who had been assisted in voting. The residents couldn't say for sure if the absentee ballot volunteers who helped them cast their ballots had done so with any faithfulness. Miller was active in the Whitely neighborhood, the city's predominantly black neighborhood, and had run for Muncie City Council.

In July 1991, the *Muncie Star* reported that Miller had died, so reporters at the *Muncie Evening Press* were startled when Miller showed up at the newspaper office later that morning. It turns out that Miller's twin brother, Marlin, was the person who had died; his death was erroneously reported as that of his brother, Melvin. "I was reading the newspaper while I was using the toilet and when I saw that I had died, I didn't have any trouble using the bathroom," Melvin Miller told reporters.

The real Melvin Miller died on November 3, 2010. Besides his service with the Muncie Police Department and in the U.S. Navy at the end of World War II, the obituary noted that he was an excellent cook.

Not noted, but worth mentioning, was that he was a tenacious detective.

## 12.
# THE DEATH OF INNOCENTS

"I didn't mean to do it, honey," John Haney said as he knelt next to his wife, who was lying on the floor of their two-room apartment on East Adams Street.

If John Haney's declaration was sincere, it was incongruous with his actions just a moment earlier, when he shot his wife, Ama Gene Haney, twice with a shotgun. The second blast was fired while she lay on the floor at his feet.

It was July 1956, and the Tennessee natives had been married eight years and had three children. John Haney was thirty-two years old, and Ama Gene was twenty-six. They had recently separated, and Ama Gene had two hours earlier filed for divorce from her husband, alleging abuse. She had also talked to a prosecutor about filing criminal charges.

John Haney had held her down, put his knees on her stomach and, at various times, threatened to suffocate her with a pillow or slit her throat. Taking all that into account, Ama Gene's friends and relatives were skeptical that John Haney didn't mean to kill his estranged wife. He maintained that he was aiming—at least the first time—for thirty-six-year-old Clayton South, a former roomer in the Haney home.

John Haney swore that he had aimed his double-barreled shotgun at South when Ama Gene stepped between them. Unexplained was the second shot. "I was shooting at him," John Haney said about Clayton South. "He wasn't satisfied until he separated us."

Ama Gene Haney. *Muncie Newspapers.*

After Haney shot his wife, he walked to his front door, took his wallet out of his pocket and threw it to a friend outside, asking the man to give it to his mother.

South told police alarming stories about John Haney's behavior in the weeks leading up to the slaying. Haney had told South that he was certain his wife intended to leave him. He planned to kill his wife and then himself, Haney reportedly told South. "I'm going to run a knife down her throat," South recounted Haney saying.

Haney went on trial in December 1956 and was found guilty of second-degree murder. The judge in the case sentenced him to life in prison. But Haney was only fifty-one when, in September 1975, he was granted clemency by Governor Otis Bowen, making him eligible for parole if he agreed to mental health treatment. Haney asked to be returned to his native Tennessee if granted parole.

ONE NEWSPAPER ACCOUNT OF the fatal shooting of Jerry Vick by Robert Turney in October 1956 called the crime "fantastically senseless." It's hard to argue with that description, considering that Jerry Vick was eleven years old and a sixth-grader at Roosevelt Elementary School when twenty-eight-year-old Turney shot him to death with a rifle while the boy watched television with his mother and his aunt in their South Vine Street home.

A week before the shooting, Turney had a threatening message for Jerry Vick, which he delivered to the boy's younger brother. "If Jerry doesn't stop throwing rocks at my kids, I'm going to shoot him," young Danny Vick recounted Turney telling him.

Turney's wife, Wilma, had gone to the Vick home to use the telephone. Robert Turney then came into the Vick home, armed with a rifle, and spoke with his wife before shooting Jerry Vick in the back twice as he sat on a couch.

Robert Turney went back to his home after the shooting, and police found him slumped in a chair. But when officers arrived, Turney—described in newspapers as a six-foot-four, 220-pound laborer—jumped to his feet and started fighting officers. He was "slugged into submission with a blackjack."

Wilma Turney had been using the Vicks' telephone to report that her husband's car had been stolen from the glass plant where he worked. But a couple of hours after the shooting, police found Robert Turney's car parked right where he had left it.

Turney had been treated two years before the slaying for a "mental disorder," but his wife said he was well when he was released. "I believe he was steadily deteriorating," coroner Eugene Eissman said.

Turney went on trial in March 1959 and was found not guilty of second-degree murder by reason of insanity. He was returned to the state hospital where he had been held for the more than two years since his arrest.

In February 1972, Delaware Circuit Court judge Alva Cox dismissed a second-degree murder charge that was still on the books and committed Turney to a mental institution for the rest of his life. Turney ended up institutionalized in Arkansas.


"MATRICIDE" IS A WORD that rarely appeared in Muncie headlines. But in November 1959, police arrested fifty-five-year-old Marshall Howard Vannatter in the slaying death of his mother, eighty-one-year-old Mary Jane Long. Police said Vannatter killed his mother with a hammer while she slept. Vannatter was convicted of the slaying and sentenced to life in prison in 1960, but in October 1965, he walked away from a prison farm at the Michigan City state prison.

A *Muncie Evening Press* writer, who plainly enjoyed holding Vannatter up to ridicule, wrote, "A Muncie lifer who experienced a little more than 24 hours of freedom was back in his cell at Michigan City state prison today with sore feet and a dim outlook on his future." Vannatter surrendered at a truck stop and complained that his feet were so sore he couldn't continue walking.


ALL DEATHS ARE TRAGIC to someone, but the death of one young man has lived on to become Muncie legend—and a mystery to some.

On July 9, 1931, a skeleton was found at the bottom of an air vent shaft at Central High School. The discovery provided answers to a question that had lingered since just before December 1922: What happened to fifteen-year-old Perlie Hogg? He had disappeared on December 21, 1922.

Perlie Hogg. *Ball State University Digital Archives.*

Born in Illinois, Perlie had led a life that was tragic from even before it began. His father left before Perlie was born, and his mother died when he was two. The child was sent to live with his aunt Minnie Cooper, who lived in Muncie. He was, as Lee Gerhart wrote in the *Muncie Evening Press* in February 1992, an unhappy boy who talked about running away to join the navy. He worked after school delivering groceries with a horse-drawn wagon and was judged a hard worker. But Perlie's mood was often dark. "Some day, you'll find me in the quarry," he told a friend about a nearby gravel pit. The implication was that he would commit suicide.

When Perlie disappeared, few noticed or, if they did notice, found it significant. Relatives in Muncie thought he had made good on his plan to join the navy.

Two plumbers, Otto Armstrong and Francis Clevenger, were working at Central, then located at High and Adams Streets, on the morning of July 9, 1931, when they found a body. Armstrong initially thought he was walking on a pile of broken bricks until he trained his light on the floor and identified skeletal remains. Coroner Clarence Piepho arrived and quickly determined that the remains were those of a teenage boy, noting that the body was wearing knickerbockers and stockings, common dress for the era when Perlie had disappeared.

Perlie's remains were ultimately identified through a rusted knife found near his body.

Although rumors persisted into the twenty-first century that Perlie was murdered and his body thrown into the shaft, authorities discounted the possibility of foul play and believed the boy had committed suicide or had died after accidentally falling into the ventilation shaft at school.

# 13.

# A MOTHER'S LOVE

**M**uncie native James A. Hedges had no bigger booster than his mother. "He was a likeable boy," Geraldine L. Greer said in December 1958 when recounting James's childhood. "Everybody liked him. He was never in any real bad trouble....I'd like the world to know he was a fine boy."

The mother's recollections came on a witness stand in a Hawaiian courtroom as her son—then a twenty-one-year-old marine private—stood trial on allegations that he had four months earlier brutally beaten and then fatally strangled a widow while stationed near Honolulu.

James Hedges had been arrested at his barracks on August 22, about fifteen hours after the discovery of the battered, partially nude body of fifty-five-year-old Helen Peoples in an alley a few blocks off Waikiki Beach. The *Honolulu Star-Advertiser* reported that the victim's "silk panties [were] found knotted around Mrs. Peoples' neck."

Hedges was linked to the slaying by a payroll check he had cashed at the Gourmet, a restaurant and nightspot where he apparently first encountered Peoples late the night before. Four witnesses would identify Hedges as the man, in civilian clothing, they later saw with Peoples on a nearby street corner.

A cab driver who early that morning had transported Hedges to the marine base, and the guards at the base's gate, all noticed that his shirt was bloody.

Frank B. Roberts Jr., a Honolulu police detective, told the *Honolulu Star Bulletin* that when awakened in his barracks, Hedges "denied any

James Hedges. *Muncie Newspapers.*

knowledge of the crime." Later, at police headquarters, Roberts said, he "reminded [Hedges] that the memory of what he had done would come back and torment him later if he didn't clear his conscience."

The detective said Hedges, "with a deep sigh…[then] admitted that he had beaten the woman and dragged her into the alleyway." Investigators—apparently from both Honolulu and military police departments—said the Muncie man then dictated an eleven-page statement that detailed the events leading to the slaying. In the confession, he allegedly admitted to striking Peoples with his fists before he "grabbed her by the throat with my hands." "I drug her back into the corner of the alley," he said. "I know I ripped her clothes off of her."

Hedges said the attack came after Peoples approached him in front of a grocery store, after their initial encounter in the Gourmet, and said something—never specified—that "blanked me off." He also reported that he had taken his victim's bracelet but later threw it into Pearl Harbor's West Loch, prompting an unsuccessful four-hour search by "Navy divers with aqua-lungs."

After providing police with the lengthy and detailed statement, investigators said, Hedges refused to sign it. Three days after his confession, Hedges was charged with murder. In keeping with a local practice, his fate would be decided by a military court-martial board, not by a jury of civilians. The maximum penalty Hedges faced, if convicted, was execution by hanging.

Before the case came to trial that December, the Muncie marine's defense counsel, Major Robert Stubbs II, tried but failed to have the case transferred to a Hawaiian territorial court. (Hawaii would not officially become a state until the following summer, on the first anniversary of the Peoples slaying.)

The prosecutor presented the testimony of the Honolulu coroner, who testified that an article of clothing had been "tied tightly around (the victim's)"

Newspaper coverage of James Hedges's arrest for murder. *Muncie Newspapers.*

neck, fracturing her larynx." She had also suffered three fractured ribs and a fractured jaw, he said. There was no indication of a sexual assault.

During the grim testimony, the *Star-Advertiser* reported, "Hedges, a 21-year-old tall, big-boned man, seemed impassive." "He yawned, rubbed his pimply brow, leaned back in his chair and picked at his uniform. Once, when a witness mentioned the dirt under Mrs. Peoples' fingernails, Hedges glanced down at his own fingers."

Stubbs tried to present testimony that called his client's sanity—and the slaying victim's character—into question. A friend of Helen Peoples was called to the stand to recount identifying the victim's remains. "Did you ever hear Mrs. Peoples called 'The Wicked Widow?'" the defense attorney asked the witness, who indicated she had not. "Would you be surprised to know that Mrs. Peoples had been arrested on the mainland as a member of a white slave ring?" Stubbs asked the woman, who responded that such information would surprise her. No testimony or evidence would follow about either allegation.

(The *Star-Advertiser* reported that Peoples—whose bombardier husband had died in the Battle of Midway in 1942—had lived in Honolulu since 1953. "In the evenings, generally wearing pedal pushers and a bare midriff top, Mrs. Peoples made the round of Waikiki bars and cocktail lounges," the story added.)

Stubbs also presented the testimony of seven defense witnesses, including Hedges's mother, from Muncie, flown to Hawaii at a cost of $11,000 to the government. The defendant's father, a Warner Gear employee also named James, said his son had always been "moody." The defendant's stepfather—who married Geraldine after James's parents divorced when James was seven years old—recalled that the defendant once kicked a television set because of poor reception.

Muncie physician Thomas Brown testified that one of the marine's grandmothers had been unstable and prone to temper tantrums. Another local physician, Forrest Kirshman, told the board he had delivered the defendant twenty-one years earlier. He recalled a head injury Hedges suffered when he fell from a playground slide as a boy, also saying that the youngster had suffered from a number of "rashes and allergies."

Two other witnesses confirmed bizarre episodes involving Hedges that his mother had mentioned while testifying. A Muncie neighbor, Thelma E. Kissell, testified that when she found Hedges in her home uninvited in January 1954, the teenager struck her in the head with a hammer, inflicting a bloody wound. She said that Hedges then looked at her and exclaimed, "For goodness sake, what happened?"

And Muncie veterinarian Richard Goodale testified that he had treated a dog, in 1955, that he was told had been stabbed by Hedges twenty-two times.

(One episode in James Hedges's past not addressed at the murder trial occurred in 1945, when a thirty-year-old clerk at the Muncie post office was charged with assault and battery in an attack on James, then seven. Newspaper accounts did not detail the allegations, and court records do not reflect how the case was resolved. Three years later, the postal clerk used a .38-caliber revolver to take his own life.)

A defense psychiatrist, J. Robert Jackson, suggested that the Muncie violence, and Peoples's killing, could have taken place while Hedges was suffering epileptic seizures. (Jackson also compared Helen Peoples to the dog stabbed by Hedges, saying she was "like a drunken puppy tangling with the wrong person.")

The prosecutor presented rebuttal evidence from medical professionals who maintained there was no evidence Hedges had epilepsy. On Christmas Eve 1958, the eight-member court-martial board deliberated for about one hour and twenty minutes before finding Hedges guilty of premeditated murder. A few days later, Honolulu newspapers noted Hedges's "dead-pan" demeanor when the board sentenced him to life in prison, also imposing a dishonorable discharge. Efforts to overturn the Muncie man's conviction began almost immediately.

Over the next two years, Hedges was returned to the mainland and confined at Camp Elliott near San Diego, with later transfers to a mental institution in Maine and a hospital in Philadelphia. In February 1961, the U.S. Court of Appeals for the Armed Forces in Washington ordered that Hedges stand trial again, ruling "too many of the court martial board which convicted Hedges had disciplinary duties as their primary responsibilities." The second trial, held at Pearl Harbor in July 1961, saw Hedges again convicted, but this time of unpremeditated murder. This time, he was sentenced to ten years of incarceration.

On June 19, 1965—two months and three days shy of the seventh anniversary of Helen Peoples's murder—James Hedges was released from the U.S. Medical Center for Federal Prisoners in Springfield, Missouri. He came home to Muncie, moving into his mother's apartment in the 1000 block of East Main Street. (When Geraldine a year earlier had divorced her second husband, she asked that her previous married name of Hedges be restored.)

Two weeks to the day after Hedges's release, a seventy-two-year-old widow named Leota Perdieu—who lived in an apartment house in the

900 block of East Adams Street, about two blocks south of Geraldine Hedges's home—was having a hard time falling asleep. About 3:00 a.m., Perdieu—who had lived alone since her husband, Walter, died in 1952—got up and poured herself a glass of orange juice.

While in her kitchen, she heard the glass in her back door shatter. Within seconds, an intruder had grabbed the senior citizen in the darkness and demanded she come with him. In her front doorway, Perdieu broke away from her captor and began screaming, running up a flight of stairs in hopes of waking the building's second-story tenants.

She didn't get far. A few seconds later, a neighbor peered out her front door and saw a stranger dragging an unconscious Perdieu down the stairs. Another neighbor, Clova Wright, saw that the man was choking Perdieu. Wright screamed, and the attacker ran away. When neighbors reached the still-unconscious Perdieu at the bottom of the stairs, they saw that a towel had been tightly wrapped around her neck. One of its ends had been stuffed into the victim's mouth.

The septuagenarian was rushed to Ball Memorial Hospital by ambulance. Her face was black and blue, and one of her eyes was swollen shut. Perdieu would remain hospitalized for several days. Her physician said she had been under treatment for a serious illness for some time before the attack.

(Perhaps Perdieu took some satisfaction when media coverage of her brush with death in all references reduced her age by a decade.)

Investigators found blood—apparently from the attacker, who had presumably suffered cuts in breaking the glass out of the door—throughout the victim's apartment.

When James Hedges was arrested on allegations that he was Perdieu's assailant, six days after the attack, he had cuts on his arms and wrists, police said. "There are several things to indicate we're on the right track," police captain David Thomas told reporters. He also noted "similarities" with the 1958 slaying of Helen Peoples.

On July 13, Hedges was formally charged with assault and battery with intent to kill and first-degree burglary. He would not, however, stand trial on the allegations that he had tried to kill Leota Perdieu. On August 9, Hedges slashed one of his arms with a razor blade in the Delaware County jail, inflicting a wound that required thirty stitches to close. He was transferred to the Norman Beatty Mental Hospital, operated by the Indiana Department of Correction in northern Indiana's LaPorte County, for "safe-keeping."

A few weeks later, Delaware Circuit Court judge Alva Cox formally committed Hedges to the state mental hospital after physicians testified that the Muncie man was "criminally insane" and not legally competent to stand trial. He returned to the Delaware County jail for about five months in 1967, but with few indications that his mental status would allow him to stand trial, local authorities eventually passed formal handling of his case on to their federal counterparts.

Hedges—accused of violating his probation in the Hawaii homicide—would spend most of the next three years in federal institutions, including the U.S. penitentiary in Terre Haute. (The charges stemming from the 1965 attack on Perdieu were finally dismissed in March 1969.)

As the years passed, Geraldine Hedges, still residing in the East Main Street apartment, awaited the return of her only surviving child. She worked at a downtown dry cleaners, worshiped at Madison Street United Methodist Church and kept active by participating in local bowling leagues.

In 1970, with parole again granted in the federal case, James Hedges was committed to Richmond State Hospital, an assignment that apparently had the support of his mother. By the end of that year, he was being granted furloughs to spend weekends with Geraldine in Muncie.

In 1971—the exact date varies in newspaper accounts—Hedges was deemed fit to return home to Muncie on a permanent basis. (In February of that year, Leota Perdieu, survivor of the brutal 1965 attack at the hands of Hedges, died at the Methodist Memorial Home in Warren. She was seventy-seven.)

In mid-November, mental health authorities alerted the Muncie Police Department that "neighbors and family" were complaining, saying "Jimmy Hedges is very mentally ill, hallucinating, laughing-screaming and [displaying] a lot of abnormal behavior." The message was meant as a warning to officers should they encounter Hedges. (A *Muncie Star* article published the following month indicated that Geraldine Hedges that month had declined to sign documents that could have led to her son's return to the Richmond hospital. "He was all she had," an unnamed source told the newspaper.)

When she left work at the dry cleaners on the late afternoon of November 29, Geraldine stopped at a downtown drugstore to look at wristwatches. At 7:14 p.m., a Muncie telephone operator received a call from a man who didn't identify himself. He said a person at Geraldine's address was in need of medical assistance. Delaware Ambulance Service personnel went to the Main Street address and found Geraldine, seemingly lifeless, on her bedroom floor. She was raced to the hospital, where she was pronounced dead on arrival at 7:40 p.m.

Authorities said the fifty-eight-year-old victim had been fatally strangled, apparently with a nylon stocking. Deputy coroner Thomas Fry said her body had "very distinctive rub marks around the neck and throat."

About 8:00 p.m., city police apprehended, without resistance, James Hedges at Main and Hackley Streets. They said he had been watching, from the street corner, the apartment he shared with his mother. Deputy police chief Richard Heath said that Hedges told officers, "I'm glad you caught me. I felt like killing others. Those voices told me to."

On December 2, Geraldine Hedges was laid to rest in Elm Ridge Cemetery. Her tombstone identified her as "Sister." Thirteen years had passed since Geraldine told the court-martial board in Hawaii, "No matter what has happened, he is my son."

James was indicted for first-degree murder, but resolution of the case would be long in coming. He was returned to the Beatty hospital in northern Indiana soon after his mother's slaying. He came back to Delaware County in August 1974, only to be "permanently committed" to the Beatty institution by Judge Cox. George Batacan, director of the Westville hospital's maximum security unit, told the judge that Hedges should "continue psychiatric treatment at the institutional level and surveillance should continue for the rest of his life."

Hedges told the judge he didn't object to the commitment. "I think I need psychiatric help," he said. "I'm not going to fight it. I want to go along with the doctors."

In September 1978, state doctors reported that Hedges had "attained sufficient comprehension to understand the nature of the charges against him [in his mother's death] and would be able to assist in his defense." He was once again returned to the Delaware County jail and pled not guilty to the murder charge by reason of insanity.

In proceedings in early December, two mental health professionals said they believed the forty-one-year-old Hedges was "psychotic" at the time he killed his mother and remained "dangerous." Cox found him not guilty of the murder charge by reason of insanity and ordered the Muncie man recommitted to the State Department of Mental Health.

This time, there would be no reprieves.

For nearly three decades, James Hedges would remain confined to a state mental facility—for most or all of that time, Richmond State Hospital. Each year, Cox and his successors on the circuit court bench would receive annual reports on the Muncie man's condition and "treatment plan." Each report prompted an "order continuing regular commitment without hearing."

(In 1982, the Muncie woman who had survived the hammer attack by a teenage James Hedges in the mid-1950s, Thelma Kissell, died in Muncie at age seventy-nine. James Hedges's father, who had relocated to Florida, died at eighty-two in 1995.)

On August 20, 2007, Delaware Circuit Court received a "notice of discharge" for James Hedges. "Commitment may be terminated," a document said. "Defendant/patient died on Aug. 12, 2007." Hedges was sixty-nine. Except for the brief periods before he had attacked Leota Perdiue in 1965 and killed his mother in 1971, he had been in custody for nearly forty-nine years.

James and Geraldine Hedges would not be reunited in death. He apparently was buried in a rural Randolph County cemetery east of Winchester, about thirty miles from his mother's resting place on Muncie's west side.

# 14.

# MURDER IN THE CLASSROOM

**L**eonard Redden was a decorated war hero.

He devoted his professional career to public education. He was a churchgoing husband and father. And—based on his actions in the final hours of his life and because of untreated mental illness—he was a cold-blooded killer, responsible for two of the most heinous slayings in east central Indiana history.

About 10:30 a.m. on Tuesday, February 2, 1960, the forty-four-year-old Redden—principal of Hartford City's William Reed Elementary School—entered the first-floor classroom of fifth-grade teacher Harriet Robson. He was armed with a shotgun.

Many of Robson's students would recall that they thought it was all a joke until Redden told their teacher, "Try to hang me, will you?" He then fired a shotgun blast into the fifty-two-year-old teacher's chest. Robson fell over a student's front-row desk and onto the floor. Her glasses fell from her face and shattered. The *Muncie Evening Press* would report that the desk, "holding a geography book and test papers, was splattered with [Robson's] blood."

Students began to scream and try to flee from the classroom. But their principal—"outwardly calm and grimly dedicated to his gruesome chore," according to the *Evening Press*—pointed his gun at the students and told them to return to their seats.

Redden then walked up a ramp to the second-floor classroom of another fifth-grade teacher, sixty-two-year-old Minnie Elizabeth McFerren. A student was reading aloud a poem—"about seashells," a classmate

Leonard Redden. *Muncie Newspapers.*

would recall—when the principal entered the classroom. "If anyone moves, I'll shoot them," he announced.

McFerren began to plead. "Leonard, don't shoot me," she said. "Don't shoot me."

As her twenty-one students looked on, Redden put the barrel of his shotgun to McFerren's head and pulled the trigger. The teacher collapsed. Her blood splattered onto a nearby piano.

As he left McFarren's classrom, Redden saw another teacher, Ralph E. Grimme, and school custodian Silas McCaffrey, who had been laying tile in a nearby hallway. Both had heard the gunfire. "I saw him come up the ramp with that gun in his hands," McCaffrey later told the *Muncie Star*. "He went to Mrs. McFerren's room and I heard her beg for her life. But he shot her."

In the hallway, McCaffrey tossed a crowbar that sailed near, but missed, the principal's head. (Blackford County prosecutor Alfred Hollander later suggested that McCaffrey's action might have prompted Redden to abandon any plans to kill more teachers.)

Grimme—a sixth-grade teacher and, like Redden, a World War II veteran—told the *Star* that the principal had "leveled the gun right at me." "I stood there for a second, then scrambled along the steps and behind the banister," recalled Grimme, adding that he then heard the principal "running down the [school's] halls."

As he left the school building, Redden encountered Esther Nesbit, the director of music for Hartford City schools, and pointed his shotgun at her. "Miss Nesbit, do you want to live?" the principal asked.

"Of course, Mr. Redden," she responded.

"Then get back in the building," Redden told her.

Outside, the principal again encountered custodian McCaffrey on the school's lawn. "I'm not going to shoot you, Si," Redden said before placing his gun in his car—a green 1952 Ford—and then driving away.

Ralph Grimme made his way into the classrooms—first McFerren's, and then Robson's—and found each of his colleague's bodies near the doorway.

Sign for William Reed School in Hartford City, Indiana. *Keith Roysdon.*

"The children were screaming and crying, and there was blood all over," he said of McFerren's classroom.

Grimme told the students to leave the school "right away" and "go home."

"You can get your coats later," he added. He briefly thought Robson might still be alive but was unable to find a pulse. Grimme and Nesbit then ran to phones in the school and called for police and ambulances to be sent to the scene.

Reed Elementary, and Hartford City's other schools, closed for the day, as did Licking Township School in southern Blackford County. (Redden was also principal of Hartford City's two other elementary schools and maintained his primary office in one of the other buildings.)

Within minutes, one of the largest manhunts in local history was underway. As many as 150 officers—not only from Hartford City and Blackford County, but also a large number of Indiana State Police troopers, deputies from Jay, Randolph and Wells Counties, and local town marshals—searched for Redden's vehicle on city streets, county roads and state highways. Roadblocks were set up at several locations. A helicopter and planes were employed in the search.

About 1:00 p.m., Delaware County farmer Ike Adams found Redden's car "mired in the mud of a thicket" about forty yards north of Delaware County Road 1200-N, a half mile west of Center Pike. The focus of the search moved to that area of northern Delaware County, where Redden apparently hunted on a regular basis.

The manhunt came to an abrupt end about 4:30 p.m. when four officers—including Randolph County sheriff Gilbert Robinson and his Jay County counterpart, George Scott—found Redden's body. He had sat down near some fallen trees in a wooded area, smoked a few cigarettes and then placed the barrel of the shotgun against his chest, using a stick to push the gun's trigger. "The pellets had blown a hole in the center of his chest," the *Evening Press* reported. Investigators believed that Redden had died perhaps as early as shortly after noon.

Those who found the body alerted fellow searchers by firing three gunshots into the air. In a short while, news photographers arrived and were apparently given full access to the suicide scene. Some papers published photos that showed the dead principal's body on the leaf-covered ground, his shotgun at his side. Others were more discreet, using photos that focused on the gun, with Redden's right hand also in view.

With the frantic search now over, authorities turned their attention to the obvious question: What had suddenly turned a pillar of the Hartford City community into a savage killer? Based on explanations from Redden's wife, supervisor and physician—in discussions both with police investigators and newspaper reporters—it quickly became apparent that mental illness and paranoid delusions had overtaken the principal in his final days. As the *Evening Press* reported, Redden was "tortured with the imaginary belief that town gossip was linking him with Harriet Robson, the fifty-two-year-old spinster teacher who was the victim of his first shotgun blast."

"He was just plain off his head," widow Hazel Redden, forty, told reporters. "He thought he was the victim of gossip. Of course there was nothing to this idea, but he couldn't throw it off. He chose to believe it, and he could not be convinced it wasn't true."

Hazel recalled that her husband first raised the purported rumor in the spring of 1959. "People are saying that you and I aren't getting along well," he told his spouse. "They're saying I'm interested, romantically, in Harriet Robson. It's not true, but they're saying it." Hazel said that she tried to persuade her husband there was nothing to be concerned about. Shortly after Christmas, however, he was again obsessed with the "gossip," she said, becoming "frenzied" about it almost every evening.

When she suggested they seek outside help, Hazel would later tell investigators, Leonard made a response that she viewed as a threat.

By Monday, February 1, Leonard Redden apparently realized that he was losing his grip on reality. He went to the office of the local superintendent of schools, E. Phillips Blackburn. Redden became emotional, Blackburn later recalled, telling his boss, "I'm sick. I'm afraid. I want you to help."

Blackburn took the principal to the office of Redden's family physician, Allen Jackson. "It only took half a look to see he was definitely disturbed," Jackson later told a reporter. "It seemed imperative that he see a psychologist." The Hartford City physician made an appointment for Redden to see a Muncie psychiatrist at 2:30 p.m. the following day.

That evening, Hazel Redden would recall, her husband seemed to be "kind of looking forward" to his Tuesday appointment in Muncie. But he remained distraught, at one point bursting into tears and telling his wife, "You've got to help me."

By now the principal believed that teacher Robson intended to sue him, and that as a result he would be in jail by week's end. Hazel agreed to go to the home of Robson—her longtime friend—who offered assurances she had no intention of suing anyone.

Leonard Redden finally fell asleep that night. Hazel did not, however, staying up to watch over her troubled spouse. She also hid all of her husband's shotgun shells that night. "I was there to protect him from himself," she later said. "I never dreamed of the other thing that happened."

On Tuesday morning, Leonard's parents—invited by their daughter-in-law—arrived from their southern Indiana home for a visit Hazel hoped would calm her husband. Hazel briefly left the house to speak with physician Jackson at his office

Leonard Redden then persuaded his father to leave also, to buy him a carton of cigarettes. After his father's departure, Redden drove to the local hardware store, where he purchased more shotgun shells. He then briefly returned home, loaded his shotgun and headed for William Reed Elementary.

There would be speculation that Leonard Redden's military service in World War II was a factor in his mental deterioration. The volunteer served with the army's Twenty-Fourth Infantry Division and saw action in the Pacific theater, taking part in major battles that drove Japanese troops from the Philippines.

He was wounded twice, in November 1944 and again in May 1945, taking part in one battle that claimed the lives of all but two men in his unit.

Redden would be awarded the Purple Heart and come home with slivers of shrapnel in one eye and a heel.

Hazel Redden told the *Indianapolis Star* that when her husband "came back from the war, he had bitterness toward people in general." In another interview, she recalled that during those last troubled nights, he had briefly referred to his military service. According to his widow, Redden told her, "You know, during the war, I killed a lot of people I didn't know just because they wore the wrong uniform. Those people hadn't done a thing to me but there are people here who have."

Post-traumatic stress and other syndromes associated with the horrors of war weren't topics of discussion in 1960, even though veterans who had seen action in World War II and, later, in Korea, were almost certainly dealing with such disorders. Even in civilian life, counseling after traumatic incidents wasn't all that common in 1960. There are no accounts indicating that students who witnessed their teachers' slayings were offered counseling at the school after the murders. (Media reports varied in the number of students who were in the classrooms when the fatal shots were fired, ranging from about forty to fifty-three.)

A Hartford City pastor did, however, give a "fatherly talk" to William Reed's fifth-graders when they returned to school on Thursday, two days after the killings.

Superintendent Blackburn told the media to stay away from the school that day. "We are doing just like we would if a teacher were absent with the flu," he told the *Evening Press*. "We brought in substitute teachers and we are trying to have normal school. We are not going to talk about what happened Tuesday.

"From here on out, our schools are going to be out of the spotlight if I have anything to do about it."

One adjustment was made as a result of the killings. The fifth-graders who had witnessed the homicides swapped classrooms with students from other grades for the remainder of the school year. Otherwise, "their eyes would go right to the spot where they last saw their teachers," Dorothy Markin, vice president of the school's parent-teacher association, told the *Muncie Star*.

Two students were recruited by news organizations—United Press International and the *Indianapolis Star*—to write firsthand accounts of the killings. A student in Robson's class recalled her fondly in his *Star* account, noting that she "didn't given us much homework." He also indicated that he had considered Redden a nice guy. "Mr. Redden pointed a gun at Miss. Robson," the boy wrote. "He said, 'They aren't going to hang me.'

Then he shot Miss Robson. All the kids thought it was a joke until we saw the blood."

A student in McFerren's class told UPI that he and his classmates were "saying poems" when their principal entered the room with a gun. "Mr. Redden says, 'If anyone moves, I'll shoot you.' Mrs. McFerren started hollering, and he put the gun right next to her head.

"She fell down by the trash can. The blood ran down her head. I looked at her and knew she was dead. We all got in the coat closet and yelled."

William Reed was closed again on Friday so that students and colleagues could attend the teachers' funerals. Robson's services were at Hartford City's First Christian Church, where Leonard Redden had been Sunday school superintendent.

Redden's funeral came on Saturday, at the same church. "We live in a hard world, filled with things that cause illness and accidents, diseases whether they be physical or mental," pastor Robert Neel told mourners. "We now consider the situation surrounding Leonard Redden, a man whose personality died before the events of Tuesday brought the death of his body.

"All of us who knew and worked with Leonard can only ask God's forgiveness that we were not sensitive to his need for help."

Redden was buried, with military honors, at Gardens of Memory Cemetery north of Muncie.

In the wake of the homicides, attorney James Emshwiller, a former Blackford Circuit Court judge, suggested "the whole community ought to be indicted for allowing a situation like this to develop." The lawyer called Redden "a potentially dangerous man, and we had to let him slaughter two fine citizens in front of children who will always carry this horrible memory.

"We don't want to hurt anybody's feelings, so we don't report to the proper authorities that someone has been acting strangely. This man should have been given medical aid. Now it's too late."

That drew a response from William Groves, president of the Blackford County Association for Mental Health. "People should not be blamed for trying to do what they think is best," Groves said. "Residents of any other Indiana community would have acted the same way under the circumstances."

"If there was anything wrong with [Redden], he kept it to himself," said school board member Joe Bonham.

After her husband's death, Hazel Redden, also a teacher, told a reporter that she had no choice but to "go on" and raise her two sons who were now without a father. "I don't know what else to do," she said. "I have the boys to take care of." Hazel taught for forty years before retiring; she died at age eighty-four in 1982.

E. Phillips Blackburn, the superintendent who sought to restore normalcy to William Reed Elementary the week of the slayings, retired in 1966. He was seventy-two when he died in 1974.

Ralph E. Grimme, who found the bodies of his teaching colleagues in the immediate wake of the gunfire, was appointed as Redden's successor as principal of William Reed Elementary. Grimme died, at seventy-two, in 1979.

Silas McCaffrey Sr., who threw a crowbar at a gun-toting Leonard Redden, was head of the maintenance department for Hartford City schools when he died of a heart attack in 1966. He was fifty-six.

Esther Nesbit, the music instructor who that bloody day assured Redden she wanted to live, left Hartford City schools in 1971. She was seventy-nine when she died in Texas in 1986.

William Reed Elementary School, which had opened in 1928, was closed in 1999. After remodeling, it reopened a few years later as Hartford Square Apartments.

In February 2015—three days after the fifty-fifth anniversary of the teachers' killings—the building was again the scene of a double homicide. Police said a Portland resident motivated by jealousy shot to death a man he viewed as his romantic rival and also killed that victim's fourteen-year-old daughter.

## 15.

# LIFE IS CHEAP

**M**urder is always shocking. It's even more shocking when it is committed over a trivial matter.

Especially when it's as trivial as a fifteen-cent loan.

Muncie's murder landscape is dotted with crimes of passion and crimes of malice and forethought. Some of the landmarks along that landscape prove only one thing: Life is cheap.

The headlines were big and bold in November 1952. "MUNCIE GROCER IS MURDERED IN STRUGGLE WITH BURGLAR" read the headline in the *Muncie Evening Press*.

Lewis Laveck, a seventy-two-year-old grocer, was found choked to death in the East Twelfth Street building that served as both his home and grocery store. Laveck's body was discovered, facedown on the blood-splattered linoleum of the small grocery, by fifty-six-year-old Carlos Morton, a Ball State University custodian who shared Laveck's living quarters.

Morton said he was asleep and didn't hear the fight between Laveck and his assailant, during which the grocer was "beaten about the face and head with a milk bottle and several soft drink bottles that were smashed in the struggle." Coroner Eugene Eissman said that, despite the blows, Laveck's death came from strangulation.

A burlap sack had been filled with potatoes, canned goods, bacon, ham and other foods and was found a short distance from Laveck's body. Police said that made them believe that Laveck's killer had been stealing groceries but was discovered by the grocer. Although the killer might have taken up to twenty-five dollars that Laveck carried on his person, about fifty dollars kept in a cigar box nearby was not touched.

With an inclination to believe the slaying occurred after the thief was surprised, police also began looking into who might have been denied credit by Laveck. Within a couple of days, Muncie police held two suspects in Laveck's death. The two weren't identified immediately, but by early December, police identified the suspects—now three—who had been arrested: Harlan "Bud" Parks, thirty-one; Cletus William Sheets, thirty-nine; and Howard Rufus Crisp, thirty-two.

Sheets and Crisp had been the first suspects in custody, but they quickly, as a headline in the *Muncie Star* said, "put the finger on" Parks. Parks told police he was in the store and attempting to steal food when Laveck entered from his living quarters in the rear. Parks said he hit Laveck with a milk bottle. But Parks implicated Sheets and Crisp, saying they had kicked and beat Laveck after the grocer fell from the blow from the milk bottle.

After beating Laveck, the three fled to Parks's home on West Fourteenth Street, where they divided forty dollars taken from Laveck's pockets. Parks kept twenty-five dollars and gave Crisp ten dollars and Sheets five dollars. "Here, you'll need something to drink on," Crisp said Parks told him and Sheets before the three went to the Happy Home Tavern at Seventh and Blaine Streets.

Sheets and Crisp were arrested, and subsequently implicated Parks, after witnesses said they saw three men at Laveck's store the night of the murder. (Parks was no stranger to the law. He had served two years in prison after a 1951 arrest for stealing a car.)

The crime began after Parks told his cohorts that he needed to buy groceries for his mother. The three drove around town, looking for a likely place to get groceries—in any manner possible. Outside Laveck's store, Sheets later told authorities that he urged Parks against robbing Laveck. "I told Bud this old man can't afford to lose any groceries," Sheets said. "Even if your mother does need them."

Crisp told police he entered the store to find Parks kicking Laveck, who was on the floor. "Quit kicking him," Crisp said he told Parks as he watched his cohort kick Laveck in the head. "Every time you do, blood squirts out of his nose and mouth."

By February, a grand jury had indicted the men in connection with the slaying. The second week of the month, Crisp and Sheets pled guilty to manslaughter. Parks, however, did not enter a guilty plea and stood trial on a murder charge in April 1953. In his testimony, Parks blamed Crisp and Sheets for the majority of the violence inflicted on Laveck.

At one point in the trial, defense attorney Ed Dixon had Parks show what he called his "lame thumb" to prove he couldn't have choked Laveck. Dixon also had his client roll up his pants legs to show that he couldn't bend his right leg, arguing that he couldn't have kicked Laveck as vigorously as Crisp and Sheets maintained.

During the trial, which took several days, Parks's mother could be seen in the courtroom gallery, reading a book. *Muncie Evening Press* columnist Evan Owens wrote that the accused killer's mother was reading a Bible.

After the guilty pleas of Crisp and Sheets, the two received lengthy prison terms in May 1953: ten to twenty-five years for robbery and two to twenty-one years for manslaughter.

After deliberations of more than two hours, a jury found Parks guilty of second-degree murder. His mother sobbed in the gallery as the verdict was read. Delaware Circuit Court judge Paul Leffler ordered that Parks be held in the Indiana State Prison in Michigan City "for and during your natural life"—a life term.

Parks's time in prison ended—briefly—in August 1968, when he was paroled by the state. But in October 1970, Parks was arrested and sent back to prison for violating his parole. He died in 1989.

MANY OF MUNCIE'S TRIVIAL murder cases were more cut-and-dried.

Dwight Ellsworth Justice told police in the summer of 1954 that he was afraid Frank Flora would kill him. Flora had a knife and brass knuckles and had threatened him, Justice told police. An officer confronted Flora, who admitted to having the weapons. The officer seized them.

Newspaper coverage of the arrest of Frank Flora. *Muncie Newspapers.*

In August of that year, Justice was fatally stabbed by Flora while visiting Flora's former wife. The two men had fought earlier in the day, and Ruby Flora told the ex-wife, "Now we'll see who's the best man."

Flora, forty-seven, had a long history of trouble with the law, the *Muncie Star* reported. The former taxi driver had been arrested several times in Muncie and Winchester for what the newspaper termed "vehicle-taking." Flora pleaded guilty to manslaughter and in December 1954 was sentenced to from two to twenty-one years in prison. He was paroled from prison in December 1958.

WHEN LESLIE GENE THOMPSON was arrested in connection with a fatal arson in June 1977, authorities already knew him. In December 1975, Thompson was arrested and held for a few days after he was seen dropping lighted matches in a trash container at an apartment building in the 100 block of West Howard Street. Although Thompson admitted dropping the matches in the trash, authorities didn't believe he meant to start the fire that killed sixty-two-year-old Mary Gibson.

Fire investigators said Thompson had been a "spectator" at other fires and had been questioned about a series of blazes in vacant buildings in May 1976. But in June 1977, Thompson was charged with arson after a fire in the 1000 block of North Penn Street killed Quitman Jones Jr. Jones died of carbon monoxide poisoning from the blaze.

Thompson pled guilty to arson and prosecutors dropped a murder charge. In January 1978, Thompson was given a prison sentence of from five to twenty years.

AN ARGUMENT OVER A fifteen-cent loan—and a shotgun blast—shattered the celebratory mood of a birthday in Muncie in March 1962.

William E. McIntosh, thirty, and Henry "Tom" Boclair, a man who said he wasn't certain of his own age, were boarders at an Ebright Street apartment house. Boclair had attended a birthday party at a friend's house and returned to his apartment at about 2:00 a.m. when McIntosh approached him and asked if he could borrow fifteen cents.

McIntosh was persistent, Boclair said, and kept returning to ask about the loan. Boclair retrieved a shotgun from behind a dresser and pointed it at the doorway to his room. "There are two steps coming down into my

**Man Slain in Dispute Over 15-Cent Loan**

By EVAN OWENS

A birthday party ended in tragedy here early Thursday when one of the guests shot and killed a friend during an argument over 15 cents.

Slain by a blast from a 12-gauge shotgun was William E. McIntosh, 30, 613 S. Ebright St.

Police arrested Henry (Tom) Boclair, about 50, who like McIntosh was a resident of the apartment house on Ebright Street. They said Boclair admitted the shooting.

Boclair told detectives he had attended a birthday party "at Abe Taylor's house on Kirby Avenue."

He showed up at the party at about 1 p.m. Wednesday and was there about 12 hours, except for a short time when he returned home to eat.

He finally left the party about 2 a.m., returning to his apartment.

A few minutes after he got there Willie McIntosh came down the hall and asked to borrow 15 cents, according to the story given detectives. Boclair told McIntosh he didn't have it.

McIntosh was persistent and Boclair told him to go home. As the story was put together by detectives, McIntosh started down the hall toward his own apartment, but turned around and started back.

Boclair repeatedly reached behind a dresser, got out his shotgun, loaded it, and held it pointed

Henry Boclair, an illiterate laborer who isn't sure of his own age, was being held on an open charge here Thurs-

Newspaper coverage of a slaying over a fifteen-cent loan. *Muncie Newspapers.*

apartment," Boclair told police. "When Willie took the first step down I shot him."

Boclair's children, ages three, five, seven and ten, witnessed their father pull the trigger.

Boclair stepped over McIntosh and went to the next apartment, where he asked his neighbor to call the police. He admitted he didn't stop to check on McIntosh. "I knew he was dead."

Authorities pursued a murder charge against Boclair, a laborer who told police he couldn't read or write. But two months after the shooting, Delaware County prosecutor Gene Williams moved to dismiss the preliminary murder charge.

A grand jury had decided that Boclair's shooting of the persistent McIntosh was self-defense.

16.

# TO PROTECT...AND TO STEAL

**W**hen police officers are issued their badges and guns, they take an oath to protect and serve their community. Most do so...and some do so at the cost of their life.

Then there are the few police officers who take advantage of their community, who cross the line between right and wrong and become lawbreakers like those who they are sworn to protect their community from.

In the late 1960s and early 1970s, Muncie and Delaware County were rocked by a scandal that hasn't been repeated since: allegations that four police officers had crossed that line and committed criminal acts.

It was a divisive time that made some Delaware County residents sleep uneasily and made many more distrustful of the officers sworn to protect them. And it helped cement the image of crime and corruption in Muncie in the minds of residents.

The incident started as a curiosity, in March 1969, as the public learned that Muncie police patrolmen James Starkey, Robert Davis and Michael Jones were suspended from police work for twenty-nine days. Police chief James P. Carey told the Muncie Police-Fire Merit Commission that the three had waived their rights to a hearing before the merit board and accepted their suspensions. The chief couldn't have suspended the officers for longer than ten days unless either they or the commission agreed to it.

The three were suspended for conduct unbecoming a police officer and being unavailable for duty, the latter charge a result of the fact that they had stepped away from their police vehicles and were not reachable by radio. And where had Starkey, Davis and Jones stepped away to?

A night watchman discovered the three in a building at the Lions Delaware County Fairgrounds at six o'clock in the morning. The building was being rented by a local appliance dealer for a big sale. The watchman was startled to find the three officers in the building and thought something was amiss when he noticed that Starkey had taken a television set from a shelf where it had been stored. When the watchman came upon the three, he told police, he found that Starkey had taken the TV and put it on the floor.

Chief Carey was quick to point out to the merit commission that nothing had been stolen. But the patrolmen were being punished because they didn't radio in to police dispatch that they had discovered the door of the building open and gone in to investigate.

Davis and Jones usually rode in the same patrol car from 11:00 p.m. to 7:00 a.m., while Starkey wasn't due to start work until 7:00 a.m. The three had had coffee together, however, and Starkey was riding with Davis and Jones as they made one last patrol of their district. Case closed?

A few days later, Veva Peters, president of the Muncie Police-Fire Merit Commission, asked the officers to attend the next meeting of the public safety promotion and disciplinary board to "clear up aspects" of the incident. The merit board meeting was held behind closed doors with only the board, Carey, the officers and their attorneys present. After the meeting, the board issued a statement that said there was "no criminal intent" on the part of the officers, who were merely making some off-hours inspection of major appliances. But the suspensions were upheld by the board. After their suspensions, the officers went back to work.

All hell broke loose a little more than a year later.

In May 1970, Starkey, Davis, Jones and another officer, Herman Bartling, were arrested. The police chief at the time, Cordell Campbell, said that months of investigation had found that the four were involved in burglaries for "at least the last two years."

Jones quickly resigned, and the other three were suspended subsequent to action by the merit commission. "Evidence indicates there were dozens of burglaries in which the four were involved," Campbell testified in Muncie City Court. While much of the supposedly stolen property was disposed of, other pieces were found in their homes, the police chief said. The loot included a portable TV, watches, guns, golf equipment, cameras, silverware and power tools.

Cordell Campbell (*right*), Muncie police chief during a period when police officers were accused of burglary. *Ball State University Digital Archives.*

Campbell said the burglaries occurred while the officers were on duty; the looted goods were sometimes hauled away in police vehicles. The officers would enter buildings, authorities said, pick out valuable items to steal and then break a glass door or window and report that they had discovered a burglary. Campbell said as much as $5,000 in cash and several thousand dollars in merchandise was stolen by the cops. The targeted businesses included sporting-goods stores, gas stations, restaurants, car dealerships, drugstores and insurance offices. "It's an almost endless list," Campbell said.

The chief cited the many officers who conducted the investigation into their brother lawmen and said it was "a very sad thing for a police chief to announce that members of his department have been accused of wrongdoing."

Bartling, who had been on the department since 1958, had been named law officer of the year by the American Legion. Starkey had been an officer since 1963, while Davis had been with the department since 1965. Jones had just become a Muncie cop in 1968. Campbell said the four were "working as a ring" and that theft and burglary charges would be filed.

Sheriff Harry Howard quickly announced that the Muncie cops were involved in as many as twenty-four burglaries in Delaware County outside the city of Muncie. Among the unlikeliest of businesses that were hit: a dress shop.

Muncie mayor Paul J. Cooley praised the members of the city department who, unlike the accused officers, worked to uphold the law. The four cops were released on $6,000 bond each, and a grand jury was called to consider formal criminal charges.

Over the next few months, multiple burglary and safe burglary charges were filed against the officers. Davis pled guilty by November 1970 and resigned from the Muncie Police Department. Jones also resigned.

As charges were filed, more details became known about the burglaries that led to the officers' indictments. Davis told authorities about a March 10, 1969 burglary at the Champion Auto Parts store at the Southway Plaza Shopping Center. A concrete block was thrown through the closed store's window, and a money box containing $241 was taken. The officers then drove to McCulloch Park, where the money was divided and the box was thrown into White River.

Although two of the four officers had resigned, Starkey and Bartling were listed as "inactive" with the department and still being paid as the investigation and their cases continued in the criminal justice system. In fact, Starkey and Bartling won a restraining order preventing the department from conducting disciplinary hearings until their criminal cases were completed.

In the meantime, two more burglary charges were filed against Starkey in November 1970, adding to the four charges he already faced. Citing the notoriety of the crimes, judges allowed changes of venue for some of the cases to other counties.

By the spring of 1972, more than three years after the fairgrounds incident that first revealed the alleged burglary ring, the effort to remove Starkey from the Muncie Police Department was ongoing. He had been suspended with pay for two years but was still taking home thousands of dollars.

By April 1972, Davis and Jones had pled guilty and Bartling was dismissed from the police department after being acquitted of a burglary charge. More than a year earlier, in late 1970, Davis had pled guilty to second-degree burglary and been sentenced to from two to five years in prison. Eight other charges against Davis were dropped.

Legal battles continued for Starkey, with the cop winning restraining orders against the merit commission and seeking a contempt of court charge against Chief Campbell. In June 1972, the merit commission found

Starkey guilty of violating departmental rules and discharged him effective immediately. The decision was reached after midnight and at the end of a marathon five-hour meeting.

Starkey's argument had been that he had told several police officers, including Campbell and then-Chief James Carey, that a ring of police officers—not including him—had been committing burglaries. Carey and Campbell said they didn't recall ever hearing any such thing from Starkey. Several officers confirmed that Starkey had told them that other cops were committing the break-ins. "It was common knowledge around the department," one police sergeant testified; some officers said that the cops would "brag" about their burglaries at police roll call.

Starkey did not take his dismissal from the department well. He filed an appeal that was denied in October 1972. He continued to fight it until a Grant County judge upheld the dismissal in February 1975. For the most part, the officers maintained a low profile in the decades following their infamy.

When Herman Bartling died in 1996, newspaper columnist Bill Spurgeon wrote a column about him for the *Star Press*. Spurgeon called the former cop "the quintessential Munsonian" and hailed his background and grasp of Muncie history. Spurgeon recalled how reporters and cops, including Bartling, would meet at about 2:00 a.m. most nights in a back room at the Pixie Diner on South Madison Street. The group drank coffee and played euchre and gin rummy.

Bartling knew the community as only a police officer could, the columnist noted. Unwritten was the most colorful period of Bartling's career in law enforcement.

## 17.
# JULES LADURON, HIS FINAL YEARS

**T**he years that followed the Carter brothers incident were for the most part quiet ones for Dr. Jules LaDuron. Still practicing medicine, LaDuron also tended farm on several acres east of Muncie. His life with his third wife, Rena, was often quiet, punctuated by incidents like one in August 1960, when LaDuron reported to authorities that seven Jersey calves had strayed from his farm along East Jackson Street.

LaDuron's strength and physicality had always been great. Bing Crosby—not the famous singer, but a Muncie firefighter, fire chief and private investigator—once told a story about how he watched LaDuron spring into action after a neighbor was trapped under a car he was repairing after it slipped off its jack. LaDuron ran into the alley and, with his bare hands, lifted the car off the man's chest so he could wriggle free.

It was LaDuron's strength that preserved his life when, later in August 1960, he was thrown from the tractor on his farm. As he lay on the ground, stunned, the tractor circled around and ran over him, a wheel running over his chest. He was treated at Ball Memorial Hospital.

LaDuron was, by the 1960s, spending vacation time in Florida but still practicing medicine, with office hours between 2:00 p.m. and 5:00 p.m. daily at his Liberty Street office. It was the same office where the Carter brothers had been killed.

The physician still made headlines occasionally. In August 1963, he spoke out at a public meeting about changes in zoning, expressing concern with how they might affect his farm ground east of Muncie. "Nobody's got any business telling a farmer what he can and cannot do with his land," LaDuron said.

Jules LaDuron in the final decades of his life. *LaDuron family*.

Stray cows continued to be LaDuron's biggest burden. In October 1968, one of his black Angus cows got out and was struck and killed by a car.

Then, in June 1969, trouble found Jules LaDuron again.

After a series of purchases of prescription drugs by a man working with police officers, police raided LaDuron's Liberty Street office. On Saturday, June 7, Muncie police, accompanied by officers from Anderson and the Indiana Food and Drug Administration, went to LaDuron's office with a warrant for his arrest. The physician had been selling amphetamines, also known as "Christmas Trees," at the time widely prescribed as "diet pills," but not dispensing them in properly labeled containers as required by state law.

Muncie police officers and informants had made five buys from LaDuron in about a week. Anderson police were present because they believed residents of their city were buying pills from LaDuron.

Richard Heath, the police investigator in charge of the city's narcotics division, recalled in 1997 how the seventy-six-year-old doctor, who had tried to close his office door on the cops, shrugged off Heath's attempts at reason. "He was walking around his office, opening drawers, and I probably got a little complacent," Heath said. LaDuron walked toward a nearby corner of the room; Heath thought he was going to pick up the telephone to call his son. Instead, Heath grabbed a World War I German bayonet off the wall.

"He turned around and he's coming at me and I'm going at him because I see what he's got," Heath said. "I had a death grip on his arm. We rassled with him to get it away from him. There were four of us and it took all of us to get him detained. The whole time, he was trying to grab the other officers' sidearms out of their holsters."

Heath's hand was cut before the cops got the bayonet away from LaDuron and got him handcuffed.

For months and years to follow, LaDuron was in the news again as one illegal prescription case or another was filed and moved through the court system. An assault charge stemming from Heath's raid on LaDuron's office was thrown out, and in February 1970, he was found not guilty on a charge of violating the state's dangerous drug act.

Just before Christmas 1970, LaDuron was arrested on similar charges. An inmate who worked with police testified in Delaware Circuit Court about how he bought pills from the physician many times. But the inmate said he approached Michael J. "Mick" Alexander, a young county police officer who would later be a prominent Muncie attorney and Delaware County prosecutor, about trying to bust LaDuron over his prescriptions. "I decided the pills were messing me up, and if it was happening to me, it must be to others, too," the man said.

This time, a jury found Jules LaDuron guilty of selling dangerous drugs. The doctor was sentenced to 180 days in prison and fined $500. The prison sentence was suspended due to LaDuron's age—eighty-one in 1974—and health. But the Indiana Board of Medical Examiners took notice and began an investigation to determine if LaDuron should lose his license to practice medicine.

At the end of almost every newspaper story about the physician, a paragraph recounted the circumstances behind the death of the Carter brothers in 1950. The case brought other unwanted attention as well. In December 1972, LaDuron reported that drugs and records had been stolen from his Liberty Street office. The theft of inventory records prevented him from determining exactly which drugs were stolen and in what quantity.

It was the beginning of the end for Jules LaDuron's medical career. In December 1975, the federal Drug Enforcement Administration revoked his registration to prescribe controlled substances, including narcotics. The DEA said that the eighty-two-year-old doctor had falsified records, indicating he had been convicted of a misdemeanor when, in fact, he had been convicted of a felony.

In September 1976, his medical license was revoked by the state. Three state police officers said LaDuron has supplied them with quaaludes, a narcotic, upon their request and, in some cases, without physical examination. LaDuron said there was no truth to the claim that he didn't examine patients who came to him for prescriptions. Everyone who comes to his office had his pulse checked at the very least, he said.

After his medical practice ended, LaDuron kept busy, his grandchildren said in 2017 interviews. The longtime physician was strong and loved the outdoors, particularly working on his East Jackson Street farm.

On February 15, 1980, LaDuron was at his farm when he told his grandson Jules, "I'm not feeling good." The younger Jules later found his grandfather, dead, sitting at his kitchen table.

Obituaries in the *Muncie Star* and the *Muncie Evening Press* reported that he died of an apparent heart attack at age eighty-six. News articles recounted his medical practice of more than a half century and his athletic abilities. "Despite his frequent brushes with the law, [he] was praised by many friends and patients," the articles noted.

Over the years, LaDuron's neighbors remembered the doctor as a welcome presence in the neighborhood, stepping out onto his porch to call to his pit bulls and being kind to children up and down the block. "My children played with his grandchildren," neighbor Eva Mae Rhoades said in a 1997 interview. "He was just good to the kids. He sewed a few of my kids up when they needed stitches."

Heath, the longtime cop who struggled to arrest LaDuron in 1969, knew kids who knew LaDuron. "We always thought that was a haunted house and he was a spooky old guy," Heath said in 1997. "Turns out we were right."

The enduring infamy of the LaDuron name was painful to his family, grandson Jules said. The younger Jules, who in recent years operated a business locally, recalled the taunts of other schoolchildren and strange looks of adults. "When you're young, kids said something to make you mad," he said. "Over time, you learn to control your temper."

The younger LaDurons prefer to remember the grandfather they knew. "I would go with him to Canada fishing," the younger Jules said. "He would drive as far into Canada as he could, until the roads ended. He stopped at logging camps and spoke to native Canadians in French."

The family remembers the Jules LaDuron who opened his medical office early so patients could wait for him in comfort, and the LaDuron who made house calls, sometimes on horseback. "The way he ran his practice," his grandson said. "He was so generous. That's why so many people looked up to him."

Considering all of his accomplishments—athlete, medical doctor, world traveler—his grave marker in Muncie's Beech Grove Cemetery is a simple one, noting only his army service in World War I.

It's doubtful any grave marker would be big enough to properly reflect all the nuances—sportsman, physician, father, grandfather, politician, husband, suspect, focus of gossip and rumor on and off for decades—of Jules LaDuron's legend.

# BIBLIOGRAPHY

## Chapter 1

Eidson, William G. "Confusion, Controversy and Quarantine: The Muncie Smallpox Epidemic of 1893." *Indiana Magazine of History* (December 1990).
*Muncie Evening Press* and *Muncie Star*. Smallpox aftermath. Various dates, 1913–43.
*Star Press*. "Ball Brothers: Muncie Industry Had a Huge Impact Here—and Beyond." March 20, 2015.

## Chapter 2

Court documents, pre-sentence report for later LaDuron drug case, Delaware Circuit Court files, 1972.
Family interviews with Leigh and Jules LaDuron, conducted fall 2017.
*Muncie Evening Press* and *Muncie Star*. Early life of Jules LaDuron. Various dates, 1911–35.

## Chapter 3

*Burlington (VT) Free Press*. "Was He Murdered?" March 29, 1889.
Findagrave.com. "Unknown Unknown." Beech Grove Cemetery, Muncie.

*Fort Scott (KS) Daily Monitor.* "Bateman Turns Up." April 3, 1889.
*Hagerstown (IN) Exponent.* "Muncie has a Murder Mystery." April 3, 1889.
*Indianapolis (IN) Journal.* "Mystery About a Murder." March 28, 29, 30, 1889.
*Indianapolis (IN) News.* "That Mystery at Muncie." March 28, 1889.
*Los Angeles Herald.* "Bateman's Disappearance." March 30, 1889.
*Los Angeles Times.* "Diabolical Crime." March 29, 1889.
*Manhattan (KS) Mercury.* "The Bateman Mystery." March 30, 1889
*Maysville (KY) Evening Bulletin.* "That Muncie Mystery." March 30, 1889.
*Muncie Morning Star.* "Cut in Two by Train." December 18, 1904.

## Chapter 4

Findagrave.com. Ezra Allen Cole, Donald Say, Clarence C., Steakley and
Luther Clint Yates.
*Muncie Evening Press* and *Muncie Star.* "Yates Arrested in Slaying of Ezra
Cole." Various editions, November–December 1937.
*Muncie Evening Press* and *Muncie Star.* "Yates Stands Trial, Returns to
Tennessee." Various editions, March 1938.
*Muncie Star.* "Man Charged with Murder Here in 1937 Held by Tennessee
Officials." January 15, 1942.
*Nashville (TN) Tennessean.* "Luther Vaughn Yates" (obituary). February 10,
1971.

## Chapter 5

"A Crusader Against 'Krusaders.'" Digital History Project, Ball State
University, 2015.
Hoover, Dwight. *Magic Middletown.* Bloomington: Indiana University Press
and Historic Muncie, 1986.
*Muncie Star* and *Muncie Evening Press.* Life and obituary of George Dale.
Various dates, 1936–91.
*New York Times.* "George Dale" (obituary). March 28, 1936.
Smith, Ron E. "The Klan's Retribution Against an Indiana Editor." *Indiana
Magazine of History* (December 2010).

## Chapter 6

*Cincinnati (OH) Enquirer.* "Indiana Suspects Held." September 2, 1932.

*Columbus (IN) Republic.* "Former Local Man Is Facing Murder Charge." August 24, 1932.

*Indianapolis (IN) Star.* "Ijames Gets Life Term for Police Death." October 15, 1932.

————. "Officer Slayer Gets Life Term." February 28, 1933.

*Muncie Evening Press* and *Muncie Star.* McCracken slaying and search for killers. Various editions, April–May 1932.

*Muncie Evening Press* and *Muncie Star.* Suspects captured, returned to Muncie. Various editions, July–September 1932.

*Muncie Evening Press* and *Muncie Star.* Wildemann sentenced to life for McCracken killing. Various editions, February–March 1933.

*Muncie Star.* "Tribute Is Paid to Muncie Pitcher." September 26, 1932.


## Chapter 7

Family interviews with Leigh and Jules LaDuron, conducted fall 2017.

*Muncie Star, Muncie Evening Press* and *Indianapolis Star.* Various issues, September 1937–March 1946.


## Chapter 8

*Garrett (IN) Clipper.* "Licensed to Wed." April 29, 1937.

*Indianapolis (IN) Star.* "Judge Studying Gleason's Case." November 1, 1939.

*Muncie Evening Press* and *Muncie Star.* "Arrest Son in Gleason Murder." Various issues, February–March, May 1934.

*Muncie Evening Press.* "Gleason Clear of Indictment." June 6, 1941.

————. "Muncie Woman Dies After Brief Illness." August 27, 1960.

*Muncie Star.* "Final Order Signed." February 10, 1961.

————. "Gleason Murder Charge Dismissed." June 6, 1941.

————. "Gleason Returned to Insane Colony." March 27, 1937.

————. "Gleason Stay in Jail to End." February 7, 1940.

————. "Gleason's Widow Free of Charge." May 18, 1934.

————. "Muncie Chiropractor Dies Suddenly at Home." May 13, 1953.

————. "Yorktown Slayer Is Adjudged Sane." December 22, 1939.

———. "Yorktown Slayer to Plead Insanity." January 12, 1940.
———. "Widow of Doctor Dies; Brief Illness." August 27, 1960.


## Chapter 9

*Chicago Tribune.* "Two Men Slain by Physician." November 7, 1950.
*Indianapolis Star.* "Muncie Doctor Slays 2." November 7, 1950.
*Muncie Evening Press* and *Muncie Star.* Carter slayings, LaDuron arrests and indictments. Various issues, November–December 1950.
*Muncie Evening Press* and *Muncie Star.* Jules LaDuron trial. Various issues, January–February 1952.
*Terre Haute (IN) Star.* "Bodies of Carters Due Here Today." November 8, 1950.


## Chapter 10

*Muncie Star* and *Muncie Evening Press.* Various articles, May 1946–January 1970.


## Chapter 11

*Muncie Star* and *Muncie Evening Press.* Various articles, December 1952–November 2010.


## Chapter 12

*Muncie Star* and *Muncie Evening Press.* Various articles, 1956–1971.


## Chapter 13

Delaware Circuit Court 1 file, State vs. James Hedges. Delaware County, Indiana.
Findagrave.com. Geraldine Hedges, James A. Hedges, Leota Perdieu.

*Honolulu (HA) Star-Advertiser, Honolulu (HA) Star-Bulletin, Muncie Evening Press* and *Muncie Star*. Hedges arrested in Hawaii slaying. Various editions, August 1958.

*Honolulu (HA) Star-Advertiser, Honolulu (HA) Star-Bulletin, Muncie Evening Press* and *Muncie Star*. Hedges faces military trial in Hawaii slaying. Various editions, December 1958.

*Honolulu (HA) Star-Bulletin*. "Pair Testify Marine Didn't Admit Killing." July 8, 1961.

*Muncie Evening Press*. "City Court News." June 13, 1945.

———. "Former City Woman Dies at Church Home." February 20, 1971.

———. "Hedges Ordered Back to Hospital." August 14, 1974.

———. "Muncie Marine Given 10 Years in Slaying." July 15, 1961.

*Muncie Evening Press* and *Muncie Star*. Hedges arrested in attack on senior citizen. Various editions, July–August 1965.

*Muncie Evening Press* and *Muncie Star*. Hedges arrested in slaying of mother. Various editions, November–December 1971.

*Muncie Evening Press* and *Muncie Star*. Hedges found guilty by reason of insanity in mother's slaying. Various editions, September–December 1978.

*Tipton (IN) Daily Tribune*. "Committed." September 1, 1965.

## *Chapter 14*

Findagrave.com. E. Phillips Blackburn, Ralph E. Grimm, Silas A. McCaffrey, Hazel Inez Routier Redden, Leonard O. Redden, Minnie Elizabeth McFerren, Harriet Robson.

*Franklin (IN) Evening Star*. "Classes Resumed at Hartford City." February 4, 1960.

*Indianapolis News*. "Pastor Appeals for 'Kindness' in Teacher Slayings." February 5, 1960.

———. "Two Hartford City Principals Named." June 13, 1960.

*Indianapolis Star*. "Former Teacher Twice Wounded." June 24, 1945.

*Indianapolis Star, Muncie Evening Press* and *Muncie Star*. Reed Elementary slayings and aftermath. Various issues, February 1960.

*Muncie Evening Press*. "Former Judge Dies After Long Illness." March 30, 1967.

———. "Named Head of Grade School." July 28, 1948.

———. "Silas McCaffrey Sr." (obituary). April 18, 1966.

*Muncie Star.* "School Supt. Blackburn Dead at 72." January 17, 1974.
*Terre Haute (IN) Tribune.* "Journey to Murder: A Long, Dark Road to Madness and Death for 2 Teachers." February 7, 1960.


# Chapter 15

*Muncie Evening Press* and *Muncie Star.* Various articles, November 1952–1989.


# Chapter 16

*Muncie Evening Press* and *Muncie Star.* Various articles, March 1969–1996.


# Chapter 17

Family members Leigh and Jules LaDuron, interviews with authors, conducted fall 2017.
Heath, Richard, and Eva Mae Rhoades, interviews with authors, conducted 1997.
*Muncie Evening Press* and *Muncie Star.* Various articles, August 1960–February 1980.

# INDEX

## A

Albany 16
Alexander, Michael J. "Mick" 117
Anderson 13, 33

## B

Ball Brothers 8
Ball Memorial Hospital 27, 43, 93, 115
Barnet, Bob 42
Bateman, Harry 22
Beech Grove Cemetery 22, 118
Benadum, Clarence 30, 52, 75
Blackford County 98
Bob's Tavern 74
Bowen, Otis 84
Brady, Arthur 12
Broderick Company 81
Bunch, Robert 9
Bunch, Rollin 9, 21, 34

## C

Campbell, Cordell 111

Carey, James P. 110
Carter, Ralph 63
Carter, Siebert 117
Carter, Siebert "Pete" 63
Cleveland Torso Murderer 54
Cole, Ezra 26
Cooley, Paul 113
Cox, Alva 85, 93
Crosby, Bing 115

## D

Dale, George 32, 45
Daleville 13
Dark Moon Restaurant 74
Delaware County 22
Democratic Party 37
Dillinger, John 47
Duerr, Edna 19

## E

Eidson, William G. 9
Elm Ridge Cemetery 95
Elwood 33

## F

Fireside Inn 72
Flyers, Muncie 18

## G

Gleason, James 56
Gleason, Lloyd 56
Griffith, Helen 79

## H

Hampton, John C 35
Haney, Ama Gene 83
Hartford City 97, 99
Heath, Richard 95, 116
Hedges, Geraldine 94
Hedges, James 88
Heekin Park 11
Henry County 18
Hogg, Perlie 85
Holloway, Lester 39

## J

Jackson, Frank 7
Jay County 100

**K**

Ku Klux Klan  32

**L**

LaDuron, Freda  49, 65
LaDuron, Jacq  63
LaDuron, Jules  15, 49, 63, 115
LaDuron, Leigh  55
Laveck, Lewis  79, 105
*Life on the Color Line*  82
Louisville  19

**M**

Magic City Tavern  76
Marion  44
Matthews, Claude  13
McCracken, James Ovid  40
McCulloch Park  15, 40, 47, 113
Middletown  33
Miller, Melvin  78, 79
Muncie High School  15
Muncie Police Department  24, 63, 94, 110
Muncie Tavern Owners Association  77

**N**

Natural gas  9
Neptune Bar  76
New Castle  18, 33
NFL  18

**O**

Oakville  43

**R**

Randolph County  12, 28, 45, 61

Redden, Leonard  97
Rivoli Theatre  42
Roosevelt Elementary School  84

**S**

Settles, Ambrose  79
smallpox  7
Southway Plaza Shopping Center  113
Starkey, James  110
Stephenson, D.C  33
Sutton, Wilbur  28, 53

**T**

taverns  72
Thorpe, Jim  16
Tipton County  40

**W**

Whitely  80
White River  22, 113
William Reed Elementary School  104
Williams, Gregory  82
Winchester  29
Wysor Grand Theatre  42

**Y**

Yates, Vaughn  26
Yates, Virgie  26
Yorktown  56
Yorktown High School  58

# ABOUT THE AUTHORS

**V**eteran journalist Douglas Walker has covered the criminal justice system in east central Indiana for most of the past three decades. For more than a quarter of a century, he has served in reporting and editing roles for the *Star Press* and its predecessor, the *Muncie Evening Press*.

Walker has received dozens of awards for writing, investigative reporting and public service from state, regional and national journalism organizations. Many have been the result of his collaborations with reporter Keith Roysdon, which whom he also co-writes a weekly column on Muncie politics. The Ball State University graduate is an eighth-generation resident of the Muncie area. Through his reporting, Walker has taken his readers to hundreds of crime scenes, scores of murder trials, two presidential inaugurations and more than thirty election nights, and into the death chamber at the Indiana State Prison for an eyewitness account of an execution.

He is married (Jennifer) and has three children and three grandchildren.

**K**eith Roysdon is a lifelong writer and journalist. He is a reporter at the *Star Press* newspaper in Muncie, Indiana, where he is the paper's watchdog reporter, covering not only the normal functions of government but also, especially, the abnormal—when things go wrong, money is misspent and elected officials misbehave.

He began earning a living in the news business when he was still in high school, and his early career included not only general assignment reporting but also entertainment coverage, including movie, book, live music and theater reviews. He began covering government in 1989 and has also covered business and economic news.

Roysdon has won more than two dozen first-place awards in Indiana newspaper contests, among them awards for community service. In addition to many awards for their work together, he and Douglas Walker won the Kent Cooper Award for story of the year in Indiana for their 2010 cold case story on Muncie's most notorious unsolved murders. Roysdon marked his fortieth anniversary in journalism in 2017. He is married (Robin) and has a son (James).